Endorsements

Sharing My Stones is a provocative insight into the epidemic of underage drunk driving. Anyone who has a teenager will read this book and immediately pass it on to their son or daughter. *Sharing My Stones* will become required reading for educators and traffic safety advocates. I could not put down this poignant account of a distinctly American tragedy.

—Denis Foley
Curator of Lewis Henry Morgan Institute-SUNY-IT
and NY STOP-DWI Coordinator-Albany County

Marianne's inspiring story shows the benefits of facing the pain of grief. The bereaved will recognize the roller coaster of emotions that she and her family experienced. Her determination that something positive would come from her son's tragic death is shown by her efforts to educate youth, parents, and school personnel on the dangers of drinking and driving. This is a message for us all, and I wish I had had this book in my hands when my daughter was killed by a drunk driver in 1977.

Sharing My Stones is a message of hope, a tribute to Matthew, and a road map for all bereaved.

—Therese S. Schoeneck
Founder/Executive Director
HOPE for Bereaved, Inc.

Marianne Angelillo gives a compelling, straight-from-the-heart glimpse of what happens to a family in the wake of a terrible tragedy. This book should be required reading for every parent—and for anyone who has ever thought there is no hope for a better tomorrow.

—Hart Seely
Author, Journalist

Thank you to Marianne Angelillo and her family for having the strength and courage to share their journey of love and loss, and to put their story into words. As parents and educators, if you truly love your children, teenagers, and students, you can't afford not to read this book.

—Joseph A. Rotella
Superintendent of Schools and Parent
Onondaga Central School District

Ali + Jake —

May you always realize the value your life holds in this world.

STAY SAFE!

Marianne
Angehll

SHARING MY
STONES

SHARING MY
STONES

MARIANNE ANGELILLO

TATE PUBLISHING
AND ENTERPRISES, LLC

Published by Tate Publishing & Enterprises, LLC
127 E. Trade Center Terrace | Mustang, Oklahoma 73064 USA
1.888.361.9473 | www.tatepublishing.com

Tate Publishing is committed to excellence in the publishing industry. The company reflects the philosophy established by the founders, based on Psalm 68:11,
"The Lord gave the word and great was the company of those who published it."

Book design copyright © 2014 by Tate Publishing, LLC. All rights reserved.
Cover design by Allen Jomoc
Interior design by Mary Jean Archival
Cover photograph by Marc Angelillo
Author photo by Laure Lillie of Skaneateles
Photos by Marianne Angelillo

Published in the United States of America

ISBN: 978-1-62854-256-1
1. Biography & Autobiography / Personal Memoirs
2. Biography & Autobiography / General
13.08.22

Sharing My Stones is dedicated to my beloved son Matthew Angelillo. Without his beautiful life, this book and journey would not have been possible.

Acknowledgements

My Family
My sister Susan
Meg Lynch
Phil Rose
Michele Whalen
Jeanette Peterson

To my devoted husband and children, thank you for always believing in me and being so patient with my long, challenging road of healing. I know it was not easy.

My sister Susan, thank you for your unending support throughout these past nine years. You cried my tears every day for the loss of our beloved Matt. You shared my son as a true godmother. You shared my grief. You took all of my stones. I am forever grateful.

My good friend Meg, you are one of the wisest women I know. Not only are you a true Christian who can look at the face of suffering, you can understand it and give such relevance to it. You have provided so much healing for me. I cannot thank you enough for the fine-tuning of my final words as you knew my heart from our many years of deep sharing.

Phil, in the midst of my suffering, you provided me an outlet to share and heal. I have learned so much through my work with you and Prevention Network. Thank you for your kindest of souls.

Michele, I met you at a crucial time in the book writing process. Your help with editing and your insight into life and education were inspirational. You gave me the courage to finish it.

To Jeanette, my fellow bereaved mother and dear friend, thank you for showing me the way to make life worth living after the death of a son.

Contents

Preface

An author friend, Hart Seely, once said that sometimes, you don't know what you are going to write until you write it. I often found that to be true as I struggled to tell our story. Even though I couldn't begin to guess who would read it, I hoped throughout its writing that some part of it would touch your life. To the teens out there, I pray you pick up this book, read it, and remember it. To the adults, I promise there will be a time when you will look back and be satisfied that you came away with a message. Good luck to myself as I write one page at a time, one chapter at a time, one day at a time. May God be with me as I ask for wisdom in putting the right words together. I am a mother who lost my seventeen-year-old son. I am on a mission to raise awareness of certain truths and realities about our culture that help me make sense of our family's tragedy. As I reflect back to tell the different parts of this story, my load has become lighter and lighter because I am *"sharing my stones,"* whether they be the heavy sorrowful ones or light, colorful ones, with you, my reader.

To write this book, I assembled the many pieces of this puzzle. They included numerous journal entries over the years, newspaper stories and articles, essays written by my family, and letters from friends and even strangers.

The task was daunting. Most of the journey I was able to remember and describe. Some of it I tell through the eyes and writings of others, often reaping what others sow. I take thoughts from books, stories, and conversations and meld them all together because that's the connector in me: sharing what I have learned, heard, and seen.

Like I used math proofs in college, I just work from step to step, one proof leading to the next. I usually cannot imagine the end result ahead of time, like how a planted garden will appear in ten years. I need the learning process—one step at a time. That's why I replant my perennials. I never can see it right the first time. That's why I read the Bible and Christian books. I cannot create the truths on my own. That's why I love photography, because I can capture the beautiful scene already there right before my eyes rather than create from nothing.

So this is the process of how I wrote this book, one day at a time, one word at a time, one page at a time.

I went through many fearful times worried that I would not be able to accomplish this task. There were so many years, weeks, days that I had to be patient and calm, knowing that each step was difficult.

I remember my friend, Meg Lynch, being impressed with how hard I was trying to do God's will and heal. She said she would never forget my response. "Well, I can say yes to just this step for right now. Then I will worry about the next step later. For now, I can just do this one little thing."

That's how my life has gone, one day at a time, one grief moment at a time, one assembly at a time, one prevention meeting at a time. I cannot put the perfect photo or image in my mind of what my life will ultimately be. I will follow the path and take one piece of wisdom, one day at a time.

> Sorrow is like holding a bag of heavy stones.
> If you give your stones out to others, your load becomes lighter.
> Hope for Bereaved, Syracuse, New York

In a Nutshell

O n Father's Day, June 19, 2004, my seventeen-year-old son, Matthew, was killed in a car crash that changed all of our lives forever. Three high school juniors left a field party in the woods where the alcohol was flowing. They piled into a red Ferrari and drove over one hundred miles per hour on a country road. The fallout from the crash and Matt's death reverberated through the homes and schools of our little town and our bigger city for what seemed like years.

Earlier that day, we were a family of six. Marc and I had been married twenty-three years and were blessed with three sons and a daughter. Our eldest son, Marc IV, at eighteen, had just finished his freshman year at the State University of New York at Albany where he played football and majored in math. Matthew had just completed his junior year in high school with a thriving and dedicated circle of friends. Alex, our fifteen-year-old intellectual ninth grader, was Matt's lifelong roommate. And our beautiful feisty daughter with red hair, Lindsay, was thirteen. We were a unit, a normal family with full hearts.

This is the story of our journey through tragedy, devastation, loss, and grief…to love, to bond, to heal, and to survive. Our story is shared in the hope that our son's life and death will have meaning and purpose. Our fervent wish is that the lessons we learned through the sorrow and pain we were dealt will save another family from a similar experience—or at least help them better cope.

Through the years, I've kept a journal. It's been both comforting and wrenching to read back over my entries. This entry reminds me of our son's great potential.

April 6, 2004

Matthew had such a huge week getting the results of his SATs, which thrilled us all. Best ever for our family tree for sure—1360! Wow! We are so proud of his dedication and commitment to this process of college prep! He really put forth his best effort preparing for this test...taking three years of Latin, reading books, studying vocabulary, and practicing every night. Hard work and determination pay off! I pray he is led to great things whatever they are! He is heading to a one-week camp at the United States Air Force Academy for an academic engineering introduction. We just have to buy the ticket to my dream place...Colorado Springs! Wow! Then off to Boys State for leadership conference.

That Night

A round midnight, the phone rings...the sound and time that transforms peace and dreams into fear.

"Hello," Marc said into the receiver.

It was Matt's friend, Matt Syers, sounding distraught.

"Mr. and Mrs. Angelillo, we are on the way to your house. Is Matt home yet?"

"No...not yet. Is everything okay?"

"I don't know. There has been an accident, and we heard there's a fatality. We have to find Matt."

Marc and I immediately sensed the urgency, realizing there was a chance our son may never come home.

Our lives were altered forever with that one call, in one night, in one instance of teenage recklessness.

That Friday night, Marc and I picked Matt up at the Syracuse Airport. We were so excited to hear about Matt's trip. He wanted to attend the US Air Force Academy and had just spent a week there for a "Summer Seminar." This was an incredible opportunity to see what cadet life would be like at the academy in Colorado Springs. While there, he called once in a panic—he'd lost his wallet. After we crossed that hurdle, the week was clear sailing. It's a wonderful feeling to just sit back and reflect upon your child's experience and feel the joy wash over you as if it is actually happening to you. This was a huge week for Marc and me, feeling that Matt was on his way to a fantastic opportunity, and that he had found himself. With his strength, intellect and guts, he could fulfill his dream and become an Air Force pilot.

Matt looked great, and we were excited to hear about everything; but it was late and we only had time to drop his bags and go to bed. It saddened me in the morning that Marc and I had to leave for a fishing derby, but we had been invited to a fabulous nature preserve with friends in nearby Savannah. We left before Matt woke up. I will never forgive myself for being so preoccupied on that day. I should have been home. I wish I had spent Matt's last day of life with him.

His day was busy, as I later heard. He had a phone call from Sandy Martin, a mother of one of his friends. She had a snake in her house, so she called the official "snake man of Skaneateles" to come over and catch it. Matt went and found it. One good deed was under his belt for the day.

Matt's sister, Lindsay, wrote about seeing him in the morning so excited, phoning his friends to explain how his week at the academy was so awesome. He was planning to go fishing on Skaneateles Lake. While we were in Savannah that day, Matt called his dad to ask if he could use our boat with his friends. Marc said yes and remembers Matt saying, "Thanks, Daddy!" in his joyful childish way.

When I arrived home later that evening, his car was in the driveway. I thought that was strange as I knew he was out. *Was he drinking then?* He usually drove his own car and was a designated driver.

Our family went to a graduation party that night. I did not expect to see Matt there, realizing he would want to be with friends. That night, there was a lot of drinking in Skaneateles. Graduation parties are big events in June. This was a big party weekend across the town. I remember Marc wanting to leave the party early with Lindsay. As designated driver, I limited my drinking and left with Alex soon after. Marc IV stayed longer. When I got home, my husband and Lindsay were snuggled up watching a movie. By midnight, we were in bed.

I heard sirens going off on my way home but thought nothing of it. Marc tried to call Matt, but his cell phone was not working. I thought back to a recent mall trip when Matt wanted to buy a new antenna for his cell phone. I remembered telling him, "Wait, we'll get it cheaper at a Verizon store." That night, we went to bed without two of our teenagers safe at home. The phone woke us up after midnight, creating a chasm of fear never experienced before in our lives. Matt's friend just told us that *someone died in a car crash*. Who was it? Could it ever be our son Matt? Where was he?

Marc and I jumped out of bed and ran downstairs to make panic-stricken calls to Matt's friends' parents, looking for the boys. Marc called a nearby hospital to ask the surreal question: had a Matt Angelillo been admitted? The terror in my heart cannot be described. The only natural thing for me to do was drop to my knees and pray the Hail Mary, beseeching our Blessed Mother to protect our son. *Please, God, let Matt be okay*.

Poor Lindsay witnessed our panic. She had never seen her parents react in this way. She saw me on my knees, praying so intently that I believe she started praying herself. She ran to her computer and put an Away message on her instant messenger account, typing, "Please don't let it be him."

Marc and I were getting no answers, so we got into the car and drove. We were stopped at the local intersection where there was confusion everywhere. Parents desperately searched for their teens, and leftover partygoers and concerned neighbors filtered through the streets. Our eldest son, Marc IV, was there, searching for his brother. My husband went to a policeman and was told to please sit and wait. Marc pleaded, "Please, my son may have been in this crash." I was waiting for Marc with some of our best friends, Ted and Kathy Kinder. Finally, the devastation began. We witnessed my strong, loving husband fall to his knees as the officer told Marc, "I am sorry Mr. Angelillo, but your son did not survive." I knew it was over; the hope to ever see Matt again was over. Marc came to tell us the news, and the Kinders later said they would never forget my reaction. In shock, I said, "We must go and tell the children."

That night, Matt and two high school friends sped off in the Ferrari from the field party in the woods. The driver and Matt were buckled in their seats and their friend sat on Matt's lap. Steven Corsello, the driver, sped in excess of one hundred miles per hour on a bend and crashed into a minivan. The Ferrari went out of control, rolled several times, and ended up in a ditch. The passenger on Matt's lap was ejected from the car and found wandering in the street. He was later diagnosed with severe neck injuries and broken vertebrae. Steven was found conscious behind the wheel and not seriously injured. A crumpled body with no response lay beside him. It was my beautiful, bright, and shining star of a son, Matt.

Matt's friend, Lizzy, later recalled that a group of friends gathered at a remote field off Dave Hull road in Borodino. They were having a great time relaxing and talking over a bonfire Matt had built. Matt was garbed in all his Air Force gear he brought home from the academy. He was ecstatically sharing his experiences. Matt had gotten a ride to this party from his neighbor and good friend, Steven Corsello.

Steven, a track star, was also celebrating his many successes of his junior year. He had been named all-state in cross-country and one week earlier, had just placed third statewide in the eight-hundred-meter run. He usually drove an old Mercedes but was encouraged by his dad to take the Ferrari because the Mercedes was not running well.

Lizzy said she tried to get Matt to go home with her because she was not drinking. She knew Steven had too much to drink, having seen him stumble. Others tried to stop Steven from driving, but no one was strong enough to take the keys. A few boys fought over who would ride home in the sports car. At one point, Matt pulled a friend out of the front seat and said, "I am going in the Ferrari!" An evening of drinking had gotten out of hand. There were not enough sober teens to control the situation.

Lizzie said she and another of Matt's best friends, Kevin, were the only two there who had not been drinking. They ended up going home together. Nobody called a parent for a ride.

It is said that the human brain is not fully developed until the early twenties. We were told Matt fought off friends for a seat in Steven's Ferrari—for "the ride of his life." Matt never would have wanted that ride unless he'd been drinking because "when you drink, you don't think." You *can't* think. All the rules and good character traits you have developed all your life go out the window when you are *under the influence*. We were told Matt said, "If I die, at least it will be in a Ferrari."

> The more you drink the more you think you can drive a car.
> Officer Robert Boris in Syracuse, NY

It is strange to recall that life-altering moment when I knew Matt was dead. I did not scream. I did not faint. I did not cry. At an intersection in beautiful Skaneateles, I simply stood there, in a strange type of acceptance, thinking, *it's over*. Matt's life is over. Matt is at peace. Matt is with God. Matt never has to suffer on this earth. Marc and I embraced our tearful son, Marc IV, in the street, and we left to go home.

The terror that evening is etched in my memories forever. My daughter says I did not cry. I stood in my home and watched the endless bath of tears. Marc IV cried hours and hours. I would just touch his arm. I remember telling Alex while he was in a deep slumber. He could not shake off the sleep to really comprehend what I was saying: that his brother, his roommate of fifteen years was…*gone*? Alex described this cataclysmic moment in an essay called "Amor Fratrium."

> I was jerked from a deep sleep one night in June of 2004. "Alex, wake up," my sister said in a panicked tone. With the dark of night and the warm comforter compelling sleep, I resisted, wanting to go back to bed. I muttered something under my breath and closed my eyes. "Alex, wake up. Matt is dead."

Reality did not set in at first. I wandered aimlessly downstairs to find a throng of people in my living room with heads buried into each other's chests. My dad came to me first. Trying to be the foundation of strength for me but failing to hold back tears and unbearable pain, he assured me intermittently through sobs that everything was going to be all right. In a blur he was followed by my mother, my eldest brother Marc, who had recently returned from his sophomore year at Albany, my sister, and dozens of friends and people I didn't recognize. Everyone said the same thing, "It's going to be okay." Somehow, that does not have as much meaning when you have every reason to believe that it is not going to be "okay." Matt was killed in a car accident that night. He and his good friend, the driver, were both drunk. Now he was gone, and nothing they said could bring him back.

—Alex Angelillo, "Amor Fratrium"

I wandered from room to room in shock as the steady stream of teenagers, friends, parents, and neighbors came, just to be with us. I just kept saying, "Matt is okay." My heart broke for everyone. I was witnessing true devastation. Marc was being so brave, answering torturous phone calls about organ donation. We would donate Matt's corneas and tissue. His body was taken from the vehicle, and we never saw him again until prepared for burial. We saw no need to have a brutal image in our mind. We stayed with broken friends who gathered at our home all night to comfort and hold each other up.

As I held each devastated friend, I would say how sorry I was. That night was a steady stream of friends. I was not ready to hear the truth of what happened. At this point, the crash didn't matter. We were just trying to digest death—that our son was *dead*? How could this be?

Marc and I found it incomprehensible that we would ever go to bed and sleep, knowing that we would have to awaken and digest the news of the death all over again. We sat out on our front porch and vowed never to sleep. A good friend promised to watch over our children while we went to bed. We held each other in a true death grip as we drifted off. In the wee hours of the morning, we resumed our positions on the front porch, listening to the morning doves. We sat for hours there, serenaded by morning doves, as visitors came to share our grief. To this day, when I hear mourning doves, a trigger of pain grabs me.

On Father's Day morning at the local annual pancake breakfast, our community would learn of our heartbreak. People told us that stunned parents hugged children while many families sat in silence unable to eat. Slowly, news filtered through the town with many arriving on our doorstep to express their condolences. I cannot recount the grief and tears that have been shed for our son. From the endless number of friends in Skaneateles to the parents of Matt's friends who watched their own children grieve and the sorrowful phone calls we had to make to our relatives, the news crushed people. Marc and I are both one of six children with large extended families. Within hours, all arrived to help us prepare for the saddest time of our lives…our final good-byes to Matt. The entire community quickly became mobilized to feed hundreds of "Matt Angelillo" grieving souls. For days, the food and helpers arrived, preparing meals for family, friends, and strangers.

Our house became a battleground fully activated with supplies including hugs, endless drinks, and meals. Later, Alex recounted the food in an essay he wrote at the United States Naval Academy.

> I think one of the most memorable things about a funeral is the food. It came from everywhere and piled high in my dining room. I guess we feel that we are missing something; we stuff our faces in order to fill the void in our hearts, but it doesn't work.
>
> —Alex Angelillo, "Amor Fratrium"

Saying Good-Bye

S ince I was a young girl, I have always had cameras in my hands. Growing up, my father was the photographer of the family. Once a month, he put on a movie night, showing us endless slides in the family living room. I took pictures in high school and college. At the University of Delaware, Marc bought me my first 35 mm camera. That's when I started my volumes of photo albums, documenting my life with family and friends. I loved to capture memories with video and photographs. Marc would ask why I couldn't enjoy a moment without having to video it. I just have a passion to capture a special event so I can always replay it.

In 2003, I bought a professional-level camcorder to videotape Matt's sport seasons. I wanted to make highlight videos for the high school football and lacrosse teams. Matt and I went together to purchase our first Mac. I remember the big decision to just "go for it!" Matt carried it out of the store and set it up on the dining room table. We learned it together. We made our first music video from a family trip to Florida. Matt so loved this computer that he purchased three shares of Apple stock for about thirteen dollars a share. He was amazed with Apple even before iTunes, iPods, iPhones, and iPads were known.

In 2003 and 2004, the new computer, filming high school sports, and making music videos were my world. Matt and I shared this because he loved it as much as I did. We would argue over music selections, which highlight clips to use, and of course, how much he should be in the video. I would put him in, and he would take himself out, saying he was only a junior and would get his chance next year. (I still put him in.) We were proud of our video for the 2003 football season. It still brings me to my knees when I hear "My Town" by Montgomery Gentry. The final lacrosse video had just been presented at the annual awards banquet while Matt was away at the Air Force Summer Seminar. I couldn't wait to share with Matt its overwhelming success and the joy I felt in creating something so awesome together.

Who would think that one week later I would be absorbed in doing a video for Matt's funeral? I felt I owed it to Matt. I wanted to celebrate his life and highlight the good times he had experienced. I wanted everyone to know what a great life he had, albeit so short. My nephews helped me rip through over one hundred photo albums and assemble the memories of seventeen great years. They stayed up most of the night to scan photo after photo for me. I used three songs that spoke to me as prayers. "Forever Young" by Rod Stewart is a song I listened to over and over for months. Images of a beautiful boy catching fish, loving friends and family, and growing up filled the screen over Rod Stewart's words.

"Everyday" by Dave Matthews Band was the song I was going to use for Matt's senior year video. He and I loved it. He suggested we save it for his graduation video. The initial lyrics hit a nerve in my heart because Matt would pick people up "every day." There were images of Matt wrapped in aluminum foil at an eighth-grade Halloween party and dressed up for the prom. Photo after photo showed Matt where he felt most comfortable, tucked in between friends.

The final song, "I Can Only Imagine" by MercyMe, brought hope and peace. One wants to imagine Matt seeing God's face for the first time and being in secure loving arms—finally home at peace. Images of Matt as part of a huge, close, loving family fill the screen. Matt was one of four siblings, twenty cousins, one hundred twenty classmates, eighteen lacrosse players, twenty-two football players, many Sherwood Inn employees, and a potential cadet at the Air Force Academy. He was so much a part of this world and poised to be a thriving member of our society.

Three days after his death, we celebrated Matt's life in the most amazing gathering of courageous, loving people I have ever witnessed. The wake had to be held at St. Mary's of the Lake Church in Skaneateles to accommodate the enormous amount of people that came. The line running out of the church was endless; the hugs and kisses we received were lifelines.

Flowers were everywhere. A prom photo of Matt graced the entrance, and I remember feeling overwhelmed by the compassion of this community. Sports teams from all over the area sent flowers, and the gift cards included the Solvay Bearcats and Syracuse University lacrosse team. A wooden stick from the legendary SU lacrosse coach, Roy Simmons Jr., adorned a flower arrangement. I guess this is what happens when a true tragedy hits. The overwhelming loss reaches so many homes via the news. A Syracuse *Post-Standard* reporter, Hart Seely, covered the crash in detail with huge headlines over Matt's handsome prom photo, "KIDS DRINK, SOMEONE DIES…A Central New York community discovers the real painful cost of drunk driving."

I remember never wanting the funeral to end. Father McGrath was amazing and inspirational as he gave meaning and purpose to a life called "eternal." What really is this eternal life? Death became this strange mystery to me as no one really knows for sure what eternal life is. There are descriptions in the Bible about a wondrous heaven. Corinthians 2:9 says, "What no eye has seen, what no ear has heard, and what no human mind has conceived— these things God has prepared for those who love him." *What really is heaven? Where are you, Matt?*

Who could really comprehend that a funeral could be beautiful and meaningful? Over one thousand people gathered to celebrate a young man's life, looking for a message to hang on to. Father ended his homily, pleading to the teens about their gifts.

> Don't waste those gifts! Don't turn them out! Don't throw them away! If anything is going to happen today by way of paying tribute to a good friend, it's got to be that we do it better. That we do better in deference to someone we love very much, to someone who has been taken from us. Know that it's the right thing to do. Know that it's the real and only tribute that we can make to this young man as we send him off to God and try to do God's work here on this earth.
>
> —Father Thomas J. McGrath

That was the message, loud and clear, to all of us that day. Make something meaningful and positive come out of this tragedy. Make Matt's life and death purposeful. Be faithful and courageous. And realize that Matt's life of seventeen years had to be enough for all of us. Marc wrote in the funeral program, "Matt's unrelenting energy allowed him to fit an entire lifetime into seventeen short years."

Our community was crushed. From friends to coaches to teachers and to our extended family, you could not house so much sorrow in one community. A special math teacher of Matt's, Tracey Bianchine, later gave us a letter she wrote to Matt.

> One of my favorite memories of you is from our eighth period class your freshman year. I was really laying into the class about something and in the middle of it I happened to look at you. You looked at me with that twinkle in your eye and devious smile and in the middle of yelling, I burst out laughing. And then so did the whole class. That's when I knew I was in for a long year. I could never stay mad at you. Your humor and ability to get a whole room going with a single smile was one of your greatest gifts. Thank you.

The other quality I liked best about you is that fire in your gut. Unlike those students who work furiously and stress themselves out, you picked what you loved and did it like no other. I can't mention this without bringing up your Regents exam. The tests hadn't even gone out yet and you made sure to get my attention so that you could signal the 1-0-0 with your hands like calling a home run. And damned if you didn't do it too! (and remind me of it every day after that!)

Your friends have all been mentioning your ability to make others feel special. I know what they mean. You did it when you stopped in to see me even though I didn't have you anymore. You did it when you insisted on having your picture taken with me at prom and made sure I kept a copy for myself. You did it when you let me lecture you about various things and you spoke to me with honesty and respect.

I guess the most disappointing part of this whole thing is it's like reading the first chapter of a good book. I was really looking forward to seeing how it was going to turn out because I knew it was going to be great! And I'm glad I got to tell you that before you left for Colorado.

I know you'll be around…Looking over your friends, watching out for Alex and your family. Just don't forget to "pop-in" on me once in a while—I still look forward to it!

—Tracey Bianchine
Skaneateles High School Math teacher

This was my first personal experience with true suffering. What does one do with it? How does one go on feeling such pain and devastation?

There is a special place on Skaneateles Lake where boats gather in a cove. You can stand on the shoreline with a view straight down the lake. It is called "the point," and it is the most magnificent view. One day, I sat at this point and wondered how many others had stood in that spot and shared its beauty. Did they suffer? My life span is short compared to all the years this lake has existed and the lives touched by its beauty. Surely I could withstand this agony and make it through my time on this earth. It could not last forever—*this suffering*. Surely I could offer it up and bear it one day at a time?

Throughout that first year, I chronicled my thoughts in a journal day and night. I would go to the lake, sit at the point, and write. I expressed my sorrow, my disappointment, and my heartache that my life had been turned upside down.

Journal Entry 6/30/04

I dedicate this new journal to the new life we have to travel without our beloved Matthew. May our memories be sweet and not painful. May the Lord bless us as we miss and love our son to such depths we never knew about before.

Clearly, my most nurturing and undemanding friend was nature. My husband later painted a picture of this healing spot. He titled it, *Mother's Mourning*. We used it for thank-you notes and had it framed. Today, it hangs in the hallway of the organization Hope for Bereaved in Syracuse.

I spent a lot of time at this healing spot, both with special people and alone. Sometimes, I would bring my dogs, my kids, my husband, or a friend or even a stranger. One friend, Lori Ruhlman, met me out there and listened with great compassion. She said later in a letter, "Your grief sounds like a trip to a foreign country where no one speaks your language." She wrote a poem to describe this meeting between a *normal* mother and a bereaved mother.

Grief was your passport
into another country; a country
you never chose to visit.
Those who have never been there
can see it from the border

and can try to imagine how it feels to live there—
but they can get no closer than tourists looking at travel
brochures.
They don't know the culture;
they can't feel the wind and the rain,
and although the language is similar,
it is spoken differently.
I have imagined, with a heavy heart, this country you are in.
Today I walked close
to try to visit you there.
You were patient with me,
a traveler who doesn't know the culture
and feels inept at speaking the language.
A gracious hostess,
you describe your country
without bitterness
towards those who do not know it.
After my visit, I realized the glory of you is this:
You are not confined to that country.
Your grief took you there,
but your passport goes both ways.
Your passport has forced you to travel
where others have not yet been
and it has given you a view of the world
and a strength to navigate
uncharted waters
while others who are sent there
might never be able to leave,
you will use your passport
to go many places.
As the years go by, you will be stronger and more able
to travel
and you will continue to make the world
a better place
just by being in it.

—Lori Ruhlman
Skaneateles, NY

Yes, the grief journey is a very lonely long one, requiring endless time and energy. Few understand it. Matt's life lasted a mere seventeen years. However, if we do the proper work, we get to keep him forever. He will forever live in our hearts, if we let him. What kind of work do we expect this to be? How can you keep a dead son alive in your heart? What is grief and where do we begin?

It would take years to sort out our devastation and anguish. Thank God we did not know what was in store for us. At times, ignorance really can be the only salvation.

The Beginnings of an Angelillo Hangout

2/2/00
Journal Entry
Matt age 13

Our family room is so full of activity. Matt is busy typing away on the computer and burning CD's. Alex is at the chess set. There is always someone at the chess set! It has been a great Christmas addition. I love to sit with Lindsay in my big new chair. I love to read or watch CNBC. Marc IV comes out of the homework room to check on us and perhaps play chess or have Matt play one of his songs. Dad hangs too. Life is good. Thank you Lord!

Marc and I made some wonderful goals while dating at the University of Delaware. I told Marc I longed for three things in our future life together. I wanted four children, a home with a fireplace, and a yellow Labrador retriever. We married in 1981, and shortly thereafter, Marc moved us to Chester County, Pennsylvania, for his new job.

We bought a home in Exton on a corner lot bordering a creek. Our house was perfect and afforded us privacy and nature. We spent years fixing it up and making trips to the local hardware store for the "honey do list."

We were blessed with our three sons and daughter while living on Glendale Road in Exton. Surrounded by friends, we loved our life there. I joined a babysitting cooperative, which gave both the children and me freedom—along with many friends.

My eldest son, Marc IV, attended a day care center up the street while I worked for Bell of Pennsylvania in the city of Philadelphia. He anxiously waited to go each morning, and he thrived with a wonderful staff of babysitters. Marc IV was the type of child who never hit or budged in a line. I used to say that he was born "sweet." He was kind to everyone, rarely getting in trouble. He followed rules, listened well, and he hugged everyone. I thought all children were like this. Then in 1987, we had Matt.

Matthew was our most challenging child. He was full of energy, extremely headstrong, but sensitive. His first words were "You dummy!" As a young mother, I felt he was exhausting at times, and I would make sure he went to bed early so we both could rest. He cried easily and wanted attention. One day, my brother's family was leaving after spending time with us, and Matt ran to the driveway and said, "Good-bye, you idiots." He had a line for everything. When my parents arrived to babysit for the week, Matt, then four, quickly declared, "You are not the boss of me." Despite his mouth, he captured hearts back then because he was so incredibly beautiful. He had the blondest hair and biggest blue eyes. They would melt your heart. His smile was contagious.

From a young age, Matt seemed attracted to girls. He loved his first grade teacher and wanted to invite her to dinner. He made sure I cooked his favorite dishes. He got dressed up and spiked his hair. He looked so handsome, the perfect gentleman. He made her feel welcome by showing her the creek and sharing his life. To this day, I will always remember Ms. Klein from Lionville Elementary School. She was one of those teachers who helped me to stay positive and to look for and nurture Matt's sensitive, sweet side.

However, I remember another teacher calling me into school because Matt insisted on helping a disabled girl too much. To a fault, he wouldn't let her do things on her own. That was Matt. He had an amazing sensitivity to girls, and it showed in so many ways.

A neighbor friend, Erin, who spent many years in the creek with my children, later wrote to me about Matt. She said, "Matt gave me a necklace for my sixteenth birthday and I kept it all these years. I just wore it on my wedding day as the 'something blue.' Matt was so special to me and I wanted to include him in my wedding day."

One of my favorite video clips is of four-year-old Matt reading *The Giving Tree*. He sees four legs under the tree instead of two and sweetly looks up and says, "He got a girlfriend!" There was such a gleam in his eye when he talked about love and girls. I wasn't surprised when Matt's first girlfriend told me later how they got married under the Skaneateles gazebo in sixth grade. They held a formal ceremony with friends to witness!

Our home in Pennsylvania gave us one of the best toys any children could have, the opportunity to catch wildlife and play in a creek. My kids would wake up in the morning and put on their creek shoes. We had endless supplies of nets, buckets, and minnow traps. I called it the "catch of the day" but demanded that all snakes, fish, crayfish, and turtles be put back by evening.

We raised ducks and would purchase at least six mallards in the spring. We herded them into a duck cage at night for safety from owls. We watched them grow and fly around the yard. In the fall, they would migrate and be gone. I will never forget the day in March when I heard quacking on my front lawn, and lo and behold, the ducks were back—waiting for the bowl of duck food I kept on the lawn. Each spring, they would lay eggs under our bushes. To this day, I am told that our old neighborhood is full of ducks.

We had an endless collection of pets. We even gave in to ball pythons, iguanas, and a corn snake. We trained Labrador retrievers for field trials, kept a pen of quails and ducks in the backyard and mice to feed Marc IV's snake, Monty the Python. Matt's prized possession was a huge green iguana, a finicky eater. Unfortunately, after his "show and tell" in school with Ms. Klein, the iguana died from lack of proper nutrition; we couldn't get the darn thing to eat. I was passionate about these animals. I even let Marc IV have a snake party, which involved pillowcases of snakes being passed around ten-year-old boys!

It was a gift to have this idyllic life and the opportunity to focus on our children. We did everything for our children, concerned with family time, safety, and teaching them the early stages of values. The good life entailed hard work, sharing time with friends and neighbors. There was never a day without a gang of dirty, muddy kids in our yard. My mini van would be packed with fishing poles, frog-catching nets, and a box of doughnuts, when we headed out for a day of nature.

Matt had a best friend, Artie, who lived two houses up the street. Artie and Matt were connected at the hip, spending hours in the creek together, catching all kinds of wildlife. Artie's mother, Judi, and I would share a cup of coffee each morning at the bus stop near my home. My family was blessed with wonderful friends, all of them actively involved in my children's lives.

The big neighborhood event was the birth of our daughter Lindsay on June 2, 1991. Friends had given me a huge baby shower, so we all were on watch for the big day. This time of year, many of us gathered at a local pool, Pennypacker, to beat the heat. The park had a great pond for fishing, and my sons were known for their nets, buckets, and poles.

The evening of Lindsay's birth, we were picnicking at the pond to celebrate Alex's second birthday. While our children helped him open his gifts, the labor pains hit. Marc and I had to abruptly leave. We had no worries about our three children as our network of friends took over. The children were divvied up with Matt, such a high-energy child, always being the "booby prize." One family, the Rubritzs, took him under their wings and adored him. It takes certain personalities to nurture the kind, gentle side of a child.

Despite how good our life was in Exton, Marc's career needed a change. In 1995, Marc was offered a job in Central New York.

We thought long and hard about leaving Chester County. But the move felt right. We researched school districts and decided to look in the village of Skaneateles.

We were first introduced to this quaint town during one of our summer trips to our hunting and fishing camp in nearby Marathon, New York, a place called Bloody Pond. We heard about this idyllic village called Skaneateles sitting on the north end of its namesake, Finger Lake, like a Norman Rockwell town. We packed a picnic, snorkeling equipment, and a huge tube, and we piled into our thirteen-foot whaler at the south end of Skaneateles Lake. We pulled the kids on a tube for about seventeen miles to the north end. We were enthralled by the unique nature of the village and lake. The water was so clean and clear, you could see the bottom. We spent the entire day investigating this lake, pulling over for a picnic and snorkeling. I could not believe such beauty existed in a short drive from Bloody Pond. It was such a perfect day that even running out of gas at the south end in Glen Haven could not tarnish the image burnt forever in my videos and in our minds.

Journal entry years later...

I remember back to our decision to move to Skaneateles in 1995. Every year I was so emotionally moved by the Christmas Dickens villages set up by a unique country garden center in Exton, PA called "Montgomerys." I would see these miniature snow-covered streetscapes, village libraries and dressed up characters walking all around downtown and I craved it. I desired to live in a small snow capped village with simple homes and people out shoveling. To add all of that and put it on a lake is heaven! And that has been what it is like living in Skaneateles!

I could not get the image of life in this Dickens-like village out of my mind. It was a difficult decision to leave Pennsylvania, but Marc had been offered a good career opportunity. We felt it was time to give the kids a smaller school district and a chance to enjoy the outdoors. Skaneateles was closer to our fishing and hunting camp. It could offer what we had always wanted, a small lake community with boating and fishing.

We were excited about the move and looked forward to a new experience. The children were between four and twelve years of age. On the wintery day that we moved, Marc IV saw me cry the entire way to New York, having said good-bye to my amazing friends. I remember how sweet and concerned he was, rubbing my back and assuring that I would meet more friends.

Journal Entry on Moving Day Dec 27, 1995
Glendale Road, Exton Pennsylvania

The last day at the house was one of the most difficult and sad times of my life. My friends showed up to help me clean the house. I felt the emotions rising all week. The thought of leaving that wonderful home and all those wonderful people that helped make all of our lives so happy and rich made it a difficult moment for all of us.

I was very blessed that the children were handling it well and especially young Marc was so strong about focusing on where we were going and not whom we were leaving.

We were all standing in my family room and one by one they were saying good-bye. I was totally speechless. Jeff Butryn said something which makes Marc and I cry every time we think about it. Jeff said, "Marianne, Marc, Angelillos…Show them in New York how to be a friend!"

Move to Skaneateles

Journal Entry January 31, 1996
Matt age 9

I wish I never had to scream again. It's been so difficult the last few days with all the kids. Matthew has been angry at the world. Last night he went into a tirade over forgetting his spelling words! He said, "I hate New York, I hate Miss Tuch, I hate my birthday party, I hate my gift. It's just a desk…It just sits there…It doesn't do anything." He went on to say he hated me, our house; his life is terrible, he misses Artie and wants to go back to Pennsylvania.

At first I was mad over the spelling words and then my heart just broke, and I could have cried. Poor Matthew, he really loved Artie, his creek, and school. I could just cry thinking of his pain.

M atthew, then in third grade, was the child in our family who least accepted changes. Thus, the transition to Skaneateles was difficult for him. He was definitely shaped by our move.

We moved during a fierce snowstorm, unpacking our house in subzero temperatures. I wondered if we were crazy. We had given the kids skis for Christmas, so we showed up at the Skaneateles ski hill with four children who had never before skied. We put them on the bunny hill. At first, they were frustrated. Of course, Matt was screaming that he stunk at it. But by the end of the day, they were all snowplowing down the slope. The Skaneateles Ski

Club saved us that first winter by bringing us so many friends. We have wonderful memories of packing picnic lunches and being outside all day. Many evenings included a potluck dinner or barbecue. This was such a great family sport to share with a community. My kids, quick studies, became avid skiers within weeks. I loved the idea of taking them away from video games and television and learning to embrace the cold and often-dreary days. I discovered a new passion for winter!

For Christmas that year, I bought Matt and Alex a K'NEX project consisting of hundreds of tiny plastic pieces, all linking together. The result would be a huge booby trap, requiring pages of diagrams to build. I thought it would keep them busy while I unpacked. They spent a week in the basement organizing the parts and then planning their strategy. They were obsessed. They spent days assembling a huge structure, which we called "The Ball." Matt brought it to school for show and tell. The teacher was so impressed, she recommended Matt for the gifted program. This amazed me, that you could become so accepted in a small school so quickly.

The first weekend after we moved, there was a knock at the door. It was a neighbor five homes up the street, Jules Corsello and his son, Steven. They had come to invite Matt to a Syracuse University basketball game. Matt bounced into the car. The Corsellos were so kind, entertaining him that night. He came home pronouncing that he had a new best friend, Steven. How fortunate we felt to have Matt gain such a friend, as he was one who wanted a buddy 24-7. Steven was into sports cars, and his dad, owner of a red Ferrari, gave Matt a red sports car toy for his birthday.

Within a month, Matt had enough friends for his first of many birthday parties in Skaneateles. This was a big deal each year, with birthdays commanding your own special meal, cake, and party. My parents had always made it a tradition to visit, wherever I lived, to bring strawberry shortcake and dinner. They always made my day special, and I wanted the same for my children.

Matt would have a house full of friends, many of whom he would invite year after year.

In the fourth grade, Matt's teacher required a three-way journal all year between Matt, Marc and I, and his teacher. This remains to be one of my favorite keepsakes because each journal entry written by Matt captures his personality so well. You realize that their personality never really changes much from this snapshot in time.

> Dear Mrs. Taylor
>
> I had a great summer, how about you? I only traveled to New Jersey twice for vacation. Then I have a cabin in Willet where I go to a lot. I went to the Skaneateles fair for two days. I like some animals but reptiles are my favorite. I have two snakes, a corn snake and a python. I play a lot of sports. My favorites are baseball, basketball, and soccer. I also play lacrosse and football. Do you play any sports? If you didn't know, I moved to New York from Pennsylvania. I am looking forward to having you as a teacher.
>
> Ps. Mrs. Clark told me to be bad
> And later…
> I'm having a great year so far. I am ready for all the tests that you are giving me this year. My favorite subjects are spelling, reading group, and writing. I hope our class can all have fun with you this year. I can't wait for it to start snowing. I also want to ice skate. Do you do any winter sports? If you ski where do you ski? I ski at Skaneateles Ski Club.
> I can't really think of anything else to say so good-bye.
>
> Love, Matt
>
> —Matt Angelillo
> Fourth grade journal entry

The move to Skaneateles was not without difficulty. We were trying to make our way into the community, looking for people we would eventually call friends. We realized that in order to fit in, you needed to play ice hockey. Clearly, new skills needed to be learned, so we started learning to skate. Our first trip to the hockey rink was humbling as we struggled to stand while our peers zipped around us. I cringed when I saw Matt sitting on the ice, wanting to take off his skates because he refused to be humiliated. I said, "Come on, Matt, don't give up!"

By the end of the day, he could manage a loop around the rink without falling. In no time, he was part of his hockey buddies' world. He loved this new life in the rink. The children could walk there every day after school for open skate. I thought I had died and gone to heaven! This new community was a dream to me, offering so much for our children.

We soon turned into a hockey family. Matt took it up right away, trying to catch up with friends who had been skating since five. I will never forget how happy he was to be dropped off to practice. He loved the sport. These are some of my favorite memories. We would travel with the children to away games including an annual trip to Ottawa, Canada. I loved the camaraderie. The players did everything together, from knee hockey in the hotel halls to eating meals. It was a unique bonding experience, which fit perfectly with Matt's personality. He was a natural leader on the ice and was high scorer for his house teams. Matt was quick on his feet with a natural gift to go to the goal. I videotaped many games simply because I loved to watch him play.

Journal Entry
January 3rd, 2000
Matt age 13

Matt has been my upbeat, happy and outgoing child. He had a "hat trick" (three goals) at his game this weekend. He went immediately to a super bowl party. He had friends over all weekend and skied Friday night. His life never stops. He loves his friends, hockey, and the Internet. He is constantly typing, chatting, instant messaging, and

never ceases to be social in some way. He's also on the high
honor roll. Way to go Matt!!

One hockey weekend especially stands out to me. Matt tried
so hard to win a tournament in Alexandria Bay for his team. He
received two "hustler" awards for each game, but they lost anyway.
Matt was so angry he threw his trophies into the trash on the way
out of the rink. I promptly retrieved them and they still sit on his
desk today. Matt was never a very good loser.

The years in Skaneateles involved a lot of sports, friends, and
time at the local lake club. I had such a passion for the lake that
I constantly wanted to look at it, sit by it, swim in it, and take
pictures of it. Being at the lake made life peaceful and passionate—
the sports, hockey especially, the ice cream cones at Doug's Fish
Fry, the chicken Caesar salads at the Blue Water Grill—two local
hangouts—and the gathering of friends on a Friday night after
the football game. The town built a community center where a
gang of us worked out every morning with a pot of coffee to
follow. It was an idyllic lifestyle. Marc said I should not tell my
family in New Jersey how good life was in Skaneateles. I lived
through my children's lives because everything they did became
my passion too. I thought this was the ultimate fulfilling lifestyle.
I loved being a mother.

Our life, however, was not without disappointments. In tenth
grade, Matt had high hopes to make the hockey team. He had
devoted years to this sport. He had made it a personal goal to
improve his skills, get stronger, and catch up to others who had
more experience. A youth hockey coach had encouraged him
along the way. But he did not make the team and was devastated.
He put a hole in his bedroom wall. He felt the selection process
was unfair. Younger players were picked for their potential by
a coach who had decided it would be a rebuilding year. After
five years of schlepping Matt to hockey games all over the state,
I was angry too, especially since he was a leading scorer. I was

crushed and angry with the high school program. I went to a youth hockey board meeting to state my feelings. Parents and students deserved a better opportunity. It took years to get over this disappointment. Matt had many friends on the team, and it hurt both of us to walk into that rink.

My good friend, Dale, wrote Matt a note, which I found in his room years later.

> Hey Matt,
>
> I understand you must be terribly disappointed about the decisions concerning hockey. Steve and I were hopeful that this would be the year your hard work and efforts would surface and you would finally crack through the ever-present selection process. I'm sorry it did not work out the way you had wanted it to. Your family and friends ache for you. Try to see how very proud of you they are in spite of this latest letdown.
>
> Your Mom has marveled at your ability to set a goal and stay focused to your achievements; ranging from your tenacity with work, to your superb accomplishments in your studies, even recently with your extended talents carving and time shared with your Dad hunting. Matt, don't let last evening's experience wear you down.
>
> Sometimes, setbacks seem to be like leaves falling from trees. Somehow, 'things' seem to work out anyway. Hopefully each time we are a little better equipped and will benefit from life's lessons.
>
> Take care and don't let anything or anyone defeat your spirit.
>
> Dale

As Dale suggested, when one door closes, one opens. And this did happen for Matt. He became an avid snowboarder after joining the high school ski club. He went every week to attack the slopes with a vengeance. His friends have written me about his passion. One of them, Wes McClurg, put it this way:

The one thing that I will always remember about Matt was our great times that we shared at ski club; he was like my ski club buddy. Matt and I would usually spend the whole night out, only going in once in a while, while everyone else would take many more trips to the lodge. The conversations Matt and I shared on the chairlift were one of a kind conversations; they ranged anywhere from when do you want to go skiing next to what do you want to do with your life, and to little things like girls. In those fifteen-minute conversations to the top we pretty much shared our whole lives with each other up to that point.

He will always be remembered in my heart right next to my father, who is someone that is just as important to remember as Matt and someone who I will never forget. Also I hope that the snow is as beautiful in heaven and the jumps are perfect too. Matt taught me to reach out farther and try harder and harder at things. He also taught me how to be a better person and especially how to live my life and turn it into a long lasting life full of joyfulness. Thank you very much for letting me be a part of Matt's life. It was an honor to know such a down to earth person; it's hard to come across people like Matt. Matt you will always be in my heart, mind and body for as long as I live.

—Wes McClurg
Skaneateles, NY

Matt had found the right sport. He planned for it to be part of his life forever. One night he told me, "Mom, thank God I didn't make that hockey team. I never would have been able to snowboard!"

It's amazing how life works out. You can't see it when it's happening. Give it time, and you will find the reasons for so many twists and turns. The one thing I regret is not following Matt to the ski hill on those snowy cold nights to videotape him. I heard he was amazing.

We made many new friends in Skaneateles. One special one was Nan Corsello, Steven's mother. On our weekly walks, Nan and I talked about everything. We also shared someone special to both of us—Matt's younger brother Alex. For years, Nan was his piano teacher, and we were both passionate about his talent. Every week, Alex would walk to her house with his music briefcase then return with a new song to be studied. Her annual recitals were a highlight for us.

Our families also came to know each other well. Nan's father, an incredible artist from Syracuse University, painted a beautiful portrait of my four children. It still hangs in my bedroom. In 2003, Nan hired me to create a video biography of Jules's father as a Christmas gift. We drove together to Syracuse to interview this wonderful ninety-five-year-old man, and we collected the family photos and his big band music. I fell in love with the story and the family. I edited it for hours. I was thrilled to do this for Nan and Jules. Also, Jules hired me to do Steven's athletic highlight film, for his resume to colleges. I interviewed Steven's track coach and collected video clips. At one point, Jules wanted to sell his Ferrari, and he asked me to photograph it for a newspaper ad. He parked it in front of my house, and I took so many shots that the image burned in my mind. Later, it did get burned into my computer files and remains today with the "Matt" files.

Memories. There are so many of them in our friendships. For my fortieth birthday, Nan gave me a plaque. It still hangs in my house, to be seen every day. It reads,

> God hath not promised
> Skies Always Blue
> Flower strewn pathways
> All our lives through;
> God hath not promised
> Sun without rain
> Joy without sorrow
> Peace without pain.

But God hath promised
Strength for the day
Rest for the labor,
Light for the way.
Grace for the trials,
Help from above,
Unfailing sympathy,
Undying love...

As Steven and Matt grew into their teenage years, they moved into different directions. They no longer were best friends, but they remained close, the usual tides of friendship waxing and waning. Steven came to all of Matt's birthday bashes in our basement, and I visited his family on Sundays, chatting over one of Jules's great kitchen creations.

I loved this family, especially Nan. She and I shared our children, our lives, and our hearts. We attended Bible studies together. We were women of great faith who adored each other and our families. The one difference between us was that Nan and Jules did not go to social events, and they did not drink. Theirs was a "dry house" and they tried hard to discourage their children from drinking. But peer pressure would become an issue as it does for so many youth in our country today.

Siblings

Journal Entry
4/26/95
Matt and Alex age 8 and 6

Matt and Alex are two such well-matched academically competitive brothers. I believe they are lucky to have each other and especially are great bedfellows. Last night I went up to their room and Alex was engrossed in a *Goosebumps* book and Matt was writing a fiction story called "The Pencil That Could Talk." They are too funny and also very lucky to have the gifts they have of intelligence. They will hopefully utilize their gifts well and give back to society in some way. Please, Lord, help Marc and I to channel their talents and energy in a much positive manner.

Alex was born two years after Matt. For fifteen years, they shared not only a bedroom, but basically everything two brothers could experience in life. They were truly soul mates. Both of them were smart and loved to learn about everything from bats to geography, but they had to make a competitive game out of learning to keep it interesting.

Early on, I recognized an interest to read, so I taught them phonics, and they both were reading before age four. I had a game to help them. They learned their vowels to a little jingle song I made up about the sounds. We would put words into a word bank as they learned to read them. It was a fun source of entertainment to watch their progress and gradually sign out

51

more challenging books from the library about the weather, the solar system, or the outdoors. The competition morphed as they grew older. They were fierce competitors over video games. One Christmas, after unwrapping a Madden football video game, they confessed to having found it in the closet, unwrapped it, and had already played it for a week. They had mastered it. But they also encouraged each other as soul mates. I would find Alex quizzing Matt about honors biology, vocabulary, or Latin. Matt recognized Alex's unique intellectual gifts. Once, in high school, he chastised Alex for spending so much time playing video games. He said, "Alex, what are you doing? You could be number one in your class…Go for it!" Each year, they received Latin awards at the high school's honors night. I keep a photo of those events close to me, always. Matt was a huge influence on Alex's desire to excel.

Two years after Matt's death, Alex wrote in his college entrance essay:

> My brother always pushed me to not take the easy road. If when I sat down to play our favorite video game, I set the difficulty to easy, he would criticize me saying I never challenged myself. He always used to tell me that I had the ability to be the best at anything I did, and he wouldn't settle for anything less. I believe that I have Matt's constant urging for me to be the best I can and I can thank Matt for all of my accomplishments throughout high school. When I sit down to play "Halo," I set it to hard and wish we could play one more level together.

Matt and Alex also bonded through hunting experiences. One cold December morning in 2003, I went with Marc, Alex, and Matt to film a duck hunt in Skaneateles. That morning, I remember feeling envy over their chance to experience the beauty and magic of first light. Later, as a cadet at the US Naval Academy, Alex would write about "First Light," a memory with his brother and dad in the salt marsh of Brigantine, New Jersey.

August 30, 2007

In late December, somewhere in the vast network of cuts and coves of the Brigantine salt marsh, we set out the spread. My dad wades in the icy waters, maneuvering the duck boat as Matt and I try to unwrap decoy lines with frozen fingers. We motor back to our spot and set the boat in against the spartina grass which covers the entire marsh. My job is organizing the boat. I line up our Kent Fasteel shells in front of our chairs, and get my dad's duck calls out of his bag. I lift one up to my lips, the oak tastes sweet in my mouth. There we are, "reeded in" as my dad likes to call it. As we wait in anticipation, the sun, waking from a long night's sleep, slowly emerges from the horizon; the pinks and oranges of its beginnings reflect brilliance off the water. This is first light.

The first birds swing in before shooting hours, whistling softly as they alight among our decoys. Buffleheads. Peddling back and forth, they whisper with soft quacks to each other. The three of us, huddled inside the boat remain silent, all watching the birds, wondering if the pair will stay long enough. Shortly after, the two go on their way to find another group of ducks, or another group of hunters. In the distance, a black duck sounds its "comeback" call, laughing at us from its refuge. Our yellow lab, now gray in the face after ten duck seasons, pounds her tail against the deck, undoubtedly scaring off any duck within a mile. First light comes and goes with no reward. Dad calms us with stories of past magnificent shoots in the Brigantine, and assures us that there is still plenty of time. Matt and I shoot glances to the left and right, hoping to see anything in the sky. I become frustrated with the morning; if only I had known that this would be my last duck hunt with Matt, I would have enjoyed the beauty and solitude of every minute I spent with him that morning.

—Alex Angelillo
"Amor Fratrium"

Alex's piece brought back special memories. Marc cried endlessly over this beautiful essay because it touched his heart in profound ways. For many years, Marc shared the outdoors and his love of hunting with his sons. He taught them about nature, animal instincts, safety, and the importance of eating breakfast together to celebrate a hunt. What mattered was the experience, not the tallies of kill. Alex gave us one more way to remember our son. It was a treasured gift.

Our eldest child, Matt's big brother, Marc, always had to have an adjective to distinguish him from his father. He was called "Baby Marc," "Little Marc," "Big Marc," and "Marc-e" at various times growing up. Now as an adult, I title him "Marc IV" as this is how the financial statements come. Marc IV always lived up to his status as chief of the Angelillo siblings.

Matt adored his older brother and always looked up to him. Later, Matt's girlfriend, Lauren, would write, "Matthew loved everything about life and he loved his family. He looked up to his big brother Marc so much and never came out and said it but he wanted to be just like him."

Matt drew his competitiveness from Marc IV. He was determined to be as good an athlete as his brother. Back in Pennsylvania, Marc IV and Matt were always involved with sports. Marc IV originally played soccer in the fall as part of a travel soccer team. He played with many good friends thinking that this sport would follow him through high school. But the second season, he was not invited back on the travel soccer team. At age ten, it seemed like a devastating consequence. But in the end, it was a gift. One month after soccer tryouts, our family was notified that the town was starting a new Pop Warner football league. They needed a quarterback! Marc IV never looked back as he started his football career. He was a gifted athlete starring in both football and Little League baseball. Matt followed in his footsteps although just a tyke of a football player. In third grade, he played tough and loved being a part of his big brother's and father's world of football. As coach, Marc would bring the boys to practice four days a week. They bonded with their dad. I still have the football program from that year along with photos and game videos. One of Matt's teammates, Pat Devlin, eventually would play for our alma mater, the University of Delaware.

Marc IV was a great role model for Matthew, showing strength, an amazing work ethic, and solid leadership on and off the field. As a high school junior, he was voted captain of the football team. He gathered his teammates all summer for workouts to make sure they would be fit for the season. He trained by running up the Skaneateles ski hill each evening. His baseball coach, Mike Flood, awarded him the "Work Horse" Award. He took his role as captain seriously and made sure to honor the athletic code of not drinking during the season. He was a young man beloved by all. We would later receive a letter from his football coach at Albany, Coach Simpson, who wrote that Marc IV was "by far the most loved individual that I have ever had the privilege to coach."

Matt and Marc had a close-knit friendship. Matt would cheer for his brother at Albany games, and when Marc IV called home from college, Matt would be the first to grab the phone. Matt was diligent about upholding his brother's reputation. When another student beat Marc IV's record of chin-ups at the high school, Matt vowed to return the title to the Angelillo family. And he did.

Marc IV's steady temperament was always a good counterbalance to Matt's excitable emotions. He would be the first to restore order to the family when chaos would hit because he had little tolerance for Matt's temper tantrums and would frequently come down hard on him. Sometimes he would leap across tables when Matt's mouth got out of control.

However, in the end, the three boys were always together in the fields, ponds, creeks, and football fields. They all shared their dad's passions for the outdoors and would often pass on their knowledge to their friends. It started in a creek on Glendale

Road, spread to a pond on Bloody Pond Road in Marathon, and matured on a Finger Lake called Skaneateles.

To me, the male world was an interesting one. I was originally introduced to it after my brother Bert was born when I was five. Having grown up with four sisters, I was thrilled to finally get a brother. My brother Bert and I were always close. We played catch in the yard, and I went to all of his sporting events. I loved having a brother, so I knew I would love having sons. I believed I was made to be a mother of boys.

But after three boys in a row, I began to get a bit panicked that I wouldn't get to experience being the mother of a daughter. I was always close to my mother and it was a source of anxiety to think that I might miss that road in life. When I was pregnant with Alex, I asked the doctor, "This time, what are my chances of having a girl?" The answer always was, "Fifty-fifty. But if I were you, I'd watch those *My Three Sons* reruns." On Alex's second birthday, our daughter Lindsay was born. When the doctor said, "It's a girl!" Marc and I cried our eyes out, overcome with emotion for days. It was a thrilling gift. Lindsay is one of our true blessings.

> Journal Entry Mother's Day 1994
> Matt, age seven
>
> It was a nice Mother's Day. The boys all helped me in some way. Marc IV spread mulch with me, Alex set the table for dinner, Lindsay helped with the mulch (complete with gloves on), and Matthew came through at the end of the day giving Lindsay a bath and dressing her. He truly loves Lindsay so much and is such a special brother to her. I hope they always have a great relationship.

Although four years younger than Matt, Lindsay was always by his side. The two were much alike in personality and energy levels. They shared a passion for friends and were always surrounded. And Lindsay loved her brother's craziness. One day, we came home to a panicked daughter who ran us into the woods where Matt lay with a broken arm. One of Matt's friends had pulled him on a snowboard with a four-wheeler. Matt had a bad fall on a jump he had built, but only after successfully making it several times. He suffered a compound fracture, requiring surgery. Poor Lindsay was horrified. Marc and I loaded him into the back of our SUV and drove off to the emergency room. Later, he proudly sported two wires coming out of his arm, looking like a bionic man.

Lindsay always took part in their basement escapades. In hide-and-go-seek, they found endless new places to vanish. Matt once got stuck in the laundry chute. Lindsay laughed at her brother's antics like failed attempts to light a potato launcher safely as she recalls part of the grass catching on fire. She followed in Matt's shoes, playing hockey and lacrosse. She'd always be found shooting a hockey puck or lacrosse ball with him.

She enjoyed thirteen years of entertainment by Matt and his friends, but it wouldn't be fair to leave out how hard Matt was on her. He called Lindsay his "pain in the ass" sister. When she annoyed him, he would hide the computer mouse or the Xbox controller. She would rummage through her brother's drawers, looking for something to wear, as Matt screamed, "Lindsay, get out of here!" But she hung in there. On the night of the junior prom, one week before he died, Matt finally let her in as a friend. She went with him to pick up his girlfriend's corsage, and she even spiked his hair for photos. The loss of her brother would forever change Lindsay. She realizes now how close they could have been throughout life.

Matt's Pinnacle

Journal Entry 4/28/02

Last night our house was wild. Marc had Casey and Eddie over, Matt had at least six friends, Lindsay had four friends and Alex had Willie and Kress. I made calzones and cookies. I love making pizza on a Friday night in my new bread maker. Well, they all seemed to have a good time...intermixing finally! Lindsay's one friend was quite outgoing and when young Marc asked her how old she was, the response drew quite a shock from the group of boys. She said, "How old do you want me to be?"

The boys could not get over it! They always were entertained by Lindsay's friends.

I love having everyone here. A full house is something I want forever. I appreciate every day of our crazy rich life. Thank you Lord! I love my four children with all my heart and soul and I love their friends.

Our family used to joke about a comment made by one of our children's friends, Casey. He said, "When you walk into the Angelillo house, you will always find someone who doesn't live there lying on the couch and *Seinfeld* is on."

He was right. We had an open-door policy for teens; the house was always full, and in 2003, usually, they were Matt's friends.

During that football season, I would always make the boys a Crock-Pot of pulled pork for after the game. As the team videographer, I did the game films. Afterward, Matt and his friends would watch them in the basement. It was a great routine. I felt confident the kids were safe. This was exactly what I loved, being surrounded and connected by people. Matt and his friends and our family's camaraderie filled my soul.

I have always loved being with people. Relationships are my top priority in life. I probably got this trait from my father, Herb. My dad always encouraged conversation and relationship. My family would gather around the kitchen table for constant sharing, so much that it became shorthand for our family's website name, "KTT...Kitchen Table Talk."

Thus, it seemed natural that Matt's style of living mimicked mine growing up. He was so much like my dad and me. Because Matt had so many friends, in some ways, I almost felt as if I could watch his life and be satisfied in mine because he was living life like I would, to the fullest with people. He always had something going on. He was surrounded by friends. We constantly had a full house, and Matt's siblings too reaped the benefits of a full social life that Matt provided with all his friends at the house.

We finished our basement with ping-pong, video games, darts, and a sleepover room. I loved Matt's friends. I was thrilled by their companionship. They were there for each other. They always had something planned. From building potato launchers or fishing for tourists with dollar bills, to a round of golf, or a game of pick-up basketball, they were always doing something.

They could entertain themselves, not forced to rely on organized sports. The small village, one square mile in size, allowed them to travel anywhere on bike. Matt would get home from lacrosse practice, string up his golf bag on the four-wheeler, and go hit balls on the golf course. There was no sport he didn't like or didn't play.

November 2003

I dedicate this journal to Matthew. We recognize his dedication and hard work in high school. We look forward to a rewarding college experience. We look forward to maturity and personal development.

Matt's junior year was the turning point of his life. He had set his goals and was determined to go to the United States Air Force Academy. He was proud of his grades and signed up for all honors classes, including English. He had changed so much from the eighth grader who received no honors in the auditorium at the end of the year. I remember I asked why he didn't get recognized. He said, "Mom, these years don't count! Don't worry I will work hard in high school when it counts."

He proved himself and was aspiring to graduate in the top twenty in his class. One night as we were sitting in the hot tub, the place where I got most of my information from my children, Matt told me how well he was doing. He went through his courses, tests, and grades. All of the sudden, he stopped, looked at my proud face and said, "Mom, I am not doing this for you—I just want to beat kids."

That competitiveness was difficult to contain. All his friends were competing in school. His grades showed it. Matt applied for National Honor Society, writing in his application essay:

My friends and teachers know that I have input to give in conversations. I always speak up and explain my views on certain ideas and topics. I'm not afraid to believe in something, and I do not fall for peer pressure in any situation. Every choice I make comes straight from my mind with little influence from others, and I pride myself on that. I believe strongly in academic integrity; it is a problem in this school from what I've seen and I have not been a part of any insincere work. It is important to me that I be compatible with any person in this school. I do not distinguish myself from others because I probably have something in common with every kid in the school, and it is one of my best qualities that I can go up to anyone in this school and have a friendly conversation.

—Matt Angelillo
National Honor Society Essay

Early in his junior year, Matt and I met with his guidance counselor to select a list of schools he might attend. Matt was clear about his number one choice: the Air Force Academy. We drew up a list of safety schools. Later, the counselor told me he saw Matt crumple it up and throw it in the garbage. He was going to the Air Force! Later, after the tragedy, I found scribbled inside his desk drawer, "This desk is signed by Matt Angelillo, 9/11/01 on the day of the kamikaze attack on New York City; they will pay."

Most of his life, from a stubborn two-year-old to a stubborn teen, Matt was a challenge for us in many ways. He was consistently difficult and frustrating to raise. He had intensity about everything, and at times, it could cause chaos in our family. Alex reminds me sometimes how I would yell at Matt, "You are giving me a nervous breakdown!"

Journal Entry February 28th, 1994
(Matt age 7)

Matthew has had such a difficult winter with his personality. Marc and I believe the Sega video game has lead to his downfall since playing since Christmas. After all of our work to get him to love art, computer, reading and writing, Sega totally drove him crazy and made him hyper and frustrated. He can't handle it at all! I believe he became short tempered with all of us and even his friends who have literally stopped calling. We will see what happens now that we have packed it away. So far, he's been drawing, and cleaning for me! How nice! There's so much talent to Matthew and so much to give if we keep on top of him and challenge him with positive endeavors. I told Marc we have been too negative with Matthew and since we have been, he has become negative too. We need a major boost and to prop up his self esteem.

I tried so hard throughout Matt's whole life to bring out his good side. I found a journal entry I wrote to him in the fourth grade, obviously after some problem at school.

Dear Matthew,

Dad and I are very proud of your many talents. We believe you can be a good leader someday. I believe you should be a leader more than a follower. This means that people will look to your behavior to imitate. That is why it is so important to be kind, generous, and good to others. Because other friends will want to be like you and then they will also be kind and good. I hate seeing people sad or unhappy because others are not treating them nicely. If they are sometimes not a good person themselves, well others should help them to change, not make it worse and ruin their chance of being happy and apart of the "group." You know what I am talking about. I am looking for you to change this situation at school and let others follow your good behavior.

Mom
Fourth Grade three-way Journal

Marc tried hard to channel Matt's boundless energy into positive directions, such as the love of outdoors and sports. Marc shared his passion for hunting and fishing, making sure they passed safety classes and learned to respect nature. One year, Marc won a turkey hunt and fly-fishing excursion; he took Matt with him. They had a wonderful day together, hunting and fishing. Matt's picture ended up on a website for the fly-fishing tour guide, a special memory for Marc.

Marc encouraged Matt and all our children to have jobs. Having worked his entire life, Marc set a work ethic as a high priority. Matt was always washing cars, making lunches, vacuuming steps, or mopping floors. From age two, he could be seen wielding a hammer on his father's building projects. He thrived on helping Dad with chores or home improvements. Marc taught all our boys how to use power tools and carving tools. You would often find them all in the basement, building anything from a bat box to a carved duck. Marc even taught his children how to paint with watercolors.

Matt and his brothers cut the lawn at a local bed and breakfast. It was a family affair; I did the gardening, and they took care of the rest. Matt later started his first official employment as a dishwasher and busboy at the Sherwood Inn, a local restaurant. He started saving for a car. He would pedal his bike to work and come home late at night, smelling like a dish room. I would find a heap of dirty clothes in the laundry room each night. Bill Eberhardt, the inn's owner, spoke to him about the Air Force where his sons served. Soon after, 9-11 occurred, and that event solidified Matt's goal to go to the academy.

I consider Matt's junior year the pinnacle. He was at the top of his game in so many ways. From friendships, good grades, getting a season pass to Labrador Mountain, and having his own wheels, Matt was one happy camper!

He'd had many of his friends since the third grade, and I admired those relationships. And that winter, a certain girl seemed to be around all the time. Lauren and Matt started dating after he gave her a snowboarding lesson. They both took honor classes, competing in everything. This was Matt's first special girl friend, and they hung out with all his other friends. The group spent many hours at our home. The pulled pork was always on. When they were together, all seemed well for the class of 2005.

Journal Entry May 24th, 2004

Matthew has had a tough junior year but is succeeding with flying colors. He aced his SATs! I cried happy tears when he got the score he wanted! It does pay off—hard work that is. He is finishing up lacrosse which has been tough at times, requiring patience as he sits the bench so much of the time. However, he has been upbeat about the camaraderie of the teammates in general. He's helped me with the season's video highlight and I have personally enjoyed the season. I think he can be a player next year.

One major event at Skaneateles High School each year was the junior prom. In May of 2004, Matt and his friends had already been planning for months. Matt and I went to pick out his tux, and Lindsay went with him for the corsages. Steven and Matt posed for photos in my kitchen. As I was walking out the door, Matt said, "One camera, Mom, pick one. That's all you're allowed!" I couldn't decide on print film, digital or video, so I put all three cameras in the car. I took them out one at a time, to avoid attracting attention.

The group gathered for photos at a friend's home, overlooking Skaneateles Lake. Matt never looked so handsome! He and Lauren were beaming, and she looked beautiful. I was on a high, just capturing the shots. I chased them, discreetly filming from behind bushes and from distant rooms. At one point, Matt shook his head and pleaded with his eyes: *That's enough!* With Matt, you had to never overstep your boundaries. Once, on our family vacation in Oregon, he grew so sick of pulling over for sunsets and lighthouses that he took the batteries from my camera and hid them in the car.

After wearing braces for years, Matt had insisted they come off before the prom. I was amazed how handsome he was without them. I had no idea that those photos—Matt without braces— would become so important to me someday. I ended up with lots of video footage, beautiful photos, and memories. I just didn't know they would have to last a lifetime. Nor did I know that this image of Matt, smiling in his tux, would be the photo on his mass card.

The month of May was a busy time for juniors. Matt studied relentlessly for the Standard Aptitude Tests—the SATs—and even carried a dictionary in his back pocket. He and Alex had received Latin awards at the high school. They posed for a photo with their medals. We hosted a barbecue for the lacrosse team, which was heading into the sectional playoffs. The lacrosse coach, Ron Doctor, was renowned for his career, and I had just finished videotaping the celebration of his three-hundred win.

I would say at this point, Matt and I had a good relationship. We both looked forward to the future. I could step away from memories of that little boy who "drove me crazy" and see this talented, beautiful young man. We had worked like partners on the highlight videos. We had started golfing together, and Matt finally could finish a round without throwing his clubs or walking off the course, leaving me to finish. We shared hopes and dreams. He was finally maturing. Marc and I felt we had done it, channeled Matt's frustrations and energy levels, and he was on his way! I became sad about him leaving for college. Marc reminded me that he wouldn't be in our daily life much longer. In June of 2004, we were excited to send Matt off to a week of summer seminar at the Air Force Academy. I remember sending his acceptance and the payment to the program, using certified mail so nothing could jeopardize this opportunity. We all were ecstatic about Matt spending a week as a cadet. He would miss the lacrosse banquet, but that didn't matter.

I took Matt to the Carousel Mall for new clothes for the week in Colorado. He was tired and irritated, not interested in shopping, but we bought hiking boots at Eastern Mountain Sports, and other items. A new yellow tie and blue shirt took time to find. We had never bought a tie together before.

The evening was momentous. We were preparing Matt for a new adventure, the next stage of his life. I treated him to dinner and said, "Matt, order whatever you want!" He chose ribs. Over dinner, we talked. I asked, "How did I do as a mom? I want to know what you think?" He said, "Mom, you did great! You and Dad gave me what I really needed in life, my freedom! I feel like you let me do what I wanted to."

Matt said he thought my video business was really cool, even though it took so many hours. He loved what I created. He asked if Lauren could come on our family vacation to Florida next winter. He planned to include her in his life.

We left that evening content with our relationship, proud and excited for his life. The Air Force Academy was waiting. He was going to be great. We both knew it.

That final evening was a unique opportunity for mother and son to assess life. It was not supposed to be a final exchange.

Losing any child is the worst thing to happen to any family. Losing a senior in high school is uniquely painful.

Journal Entry June 18th, 2004

I am so excited about Matt coming home tonight! I think he loved the week at the Air Force Academy and wants to go there. Help it all be right!

Rite of Passage

Journal Entry 9/20/1998

We are at the cabin and I believe I never wanted and needed to get here more. We had such a shocking and disappointing episode on Saturday night and I believe there's probably a lot more to come but the official teenage problems hit home!!

We started out having our first official barbecue at the club. It was wonderful! Many different friends came with so many children and it was a beautiful night!! Everyone brought a dish to pass, boats and kayaks were available for rides, and an airplane was doing tricks in front of us. It was the most beautiful evening and so casual and friendly as all our old "Pennypacker" barbeques used to be. How I had missed that Pennypacker more than anything the last two years… Casual barbeques, friends, fun for children and good old-fashioned picnic style parties.

Well after our bonfire, all the children were doing sparklers and marshmallows, etc and we went home to put the kids to bed. Marc IV had two friends spend the night. We all went to bed and then the call came in at 4am from a policeman saying, "We have your son. He's intoxicated and we are at your front door."

Marc and I were so bewildered and confused as to what the heck he was talking about. Our son was in bed! But yet there was our son, Marc IV, and his two friends in the back of the police car at 4AM, drunk, and smelling like crap!

Marc and I were so upset and shocked. We had talked to Marc so many times about the drinking in Skaneateles and how he needs to step up and be a leader and not succumb to alcohol. We discussed his athletic abilities and how drinking could get him thrown off teams! Well so much for that! I guess teenage curiosity prevails, and it happens!

So that's why we all needed a break from life in Skaneateles and come to where life is simple, unchallenging, naturalistic, and peaceful! We have such a place of comfort and solace at Bloody Pond. God brought us to this place and said, "You need a place to regroup, think of me, and appreciate your family and your life." Lord, thanks for giving us this opportunity!

One element was threaded throughout social occasions in Skaneateles: alcohol. Marc and I cannot help but look back at the degree it played a role in our social lives. We went to Friday-evening happy hours at the country club so we could meet our friends. We put beers in our boat on a Saturday afternoon, and coolers were present at every picnic we attended. Kegs flowed at graduation parties with teens waiting to polish them off after the adults left. This included Marc IV's graduation party at our home in 2002. This was not alarming to me. We didn't see how much the kids were absorbing and learning from everything we did. I was blind to the degree that our teenagers were drinking right alongside us. I was clueless.

A few friends who grew up in Skaneateles said it had always been this way. Parents would leave for a weekend, and plans were quickly made for a beer party. It had gone on forever. It had been a *rite of passage* for teens in this community. Some parents fought it and became ostracized. Most looked the other way, thinking no harm would come from it, because they also did it when they were young. This *rite of passage* was hardly exclusive to Skaneateles. It is a plague upon every community across America.

I had never worried about my children using drugs because I had preached to them long and hard about the horrifying consequences of drug addiction. My sister had a terrible history with drug abuse. When I was in college, my parents were struggling with her back home. She suffered from depression and needed help with an addiction to drugs. I felt devastated for her as I was in a blissful college environment. I had great friends and a wonderful boyfriend. How could a sibling experience something so differently? We were raised in the same family, the same upbringing, the same parents and opportunities! How could such a thing happen to a family that was so successful and loving?

Later, my sister would tell of being bullied in grammar school and finding solace with the wrong crowd. A boyfriend offered her drugs. She ended up using marijuana. That led to stronger drugs and dangerous experiences. It affected her for the rest of her life. She drained her early retirement funds spending on drugs. She needed rehab and joined Alcoholics Anonymous, spending many years working hard in recovery. Because of this, I have always feared drugs. I basically lost my sister for years as I watched her struggle. Her recovery was long and painful and very hard on my family. My brother, Bert, who was the youngest in the family, suffered the most. Her addiction affected him forever.

My sister hid her drug use from my parents. Because it's hard to hide an addiction of any kind, I believe it was the main reason she was so isolated from the family. You must lie constantly. The act of hiding your life leads to loneliness and depression. I believe this is the saddest part of addiction.

When I was in college, I stayed away from marijuana. I always recall the drug users as different and isolated from the mainstream. I always believed marijuana was a gateway drug. I brainwashed Matt and Marc to never use pot. What happened to my sister scared me, but Matt and Marc IV reassured me that they would never use drugs. They set themselves apart from it. They warned friends it would make them lack the desire to achieve.

Sure enough, you could see the exodus from sports and activities by some of those who chose to use. They were losing passion, interest, and energy and replacing it with a drug-induced high. I could see social groups splitting apart because of marijuana.

In college, alcohol seemed more the norm and far less risky. I did not see or understand at the time that all partying with alcohol involves risk. The degree of freedom, the rite of passage to drink, and the still-maturing teenage brain is a bad combination. College bingeing is a national dilemma that is not going away.[1] There could have been bad outcomes for me from some nights of abusing alcohol, but I was lucky. I never had a predisposition to alcohol or an accident while under the influence. I hated the taste of it, and I hated being tired from it. I quickly outgrew the need to party after college and became a social drinker.

Skaneateles high school had a strict athletic code; athletes were not allowed to drink or use substances during the season. I trusted the system. I thought it worked. Of course, the off-season was a different matter. There always was a problem somewhere. At a young age, Marc IV and his friends experimented with alcohol. In a way, I was glad Marc IV was caught in that eighth-grade incident because it made us vigilant. We never condoned it. But Matt was watching closely. He and his friends were observing the behavior of older siblings. They talked about how their day was coming. Soon enough, they would be participating in the ritual.

One weekend, Matt and Steven were almost hit by a car while crossing the highway to buy snacks. A policeman stopped them. He saw that they were under the influence. The policeman asked, "Where did you get it?" Matt said, "Steven Corsello's older sister…"

Wow! That created immediate problems. The Corsello family claimed Matt stole it from their daughter, and that Steven was not to blame. I asked Matt several times if he was telling the truth. He said yes. He said he felt terrible for getting Steven's sister in trouble, but he had to tell the truth.

Nan and I discussed the situation on one of our walks. She supported her family. She challenged Matt's account. To this day, I don't know the truth about how they got the alcohol, but the fact remained that our sons were drinking. At the time, I felt the Corsellos were in denial, unable to believe that Steven drank right along with Matt. Being nondrinkers, they could not believe their son would drink. The incident stopped me from ever confronting the Corsellos again about teenage drinking.

Another incident occurred in Matt's sophomore year. A coach surprised an underage drinking party, and many students, Matt among them, accepted the punishment. The coach's own daughter was at the party. He did not hesitate to turn her in!

I asked Matt who was there. I questioned whether Steven was a drinker. Steven was an amazing track runner, headed for a scholarship. Matt alleged that Steven had climbed out a back window, escaping the consequences.

Matt later attended a drug and alcohol workshop with a student assistance counselor. He went to the sessions and had to miss a few lacrosse games. Once again, I was glad he'd been caught. I believed he had gotten the message: There were consequences to drinking.

Despite all our warnings and incidences, we wanted to trust the teenagers in our home. We continued to host gatherings and offered use of our basement. We thought sleepovers were a good thing. We didn't know that kids were sneaking alcohol into our home through a back basement door. Later, we realized that we were not supervising as closely as we should have been. One night, Marc caught a group of lacrosse players drinking in the basement. He threw them out but never told the coach—a decision he still regrets every day. We missed opportunities to force consequences and to instill change. We believed this was normal teenage behavior, so we told ourselves not to worry.

Journal entry: June 28th, 2003

We've had such an alcohol problem lately in this town. Marc IV had to go to court for a ticket of illegal possession of alcohol, his good friends were almost killed in a boating accident and another friend was in a car accident.... all under the influence. *It needs to stop!* I hope they all survive these binges. It just seems its unnecessary to drink excessively like they do and many start at thirteen in this town.

A few months into Matt's junior year, I received a call from Dr. Barbara Connor, a parent of one of Matt's friends. She was alarmed at the use of alcohol by the youngsters. She felt we needed to gather as parents and discuss what to do. Ironically, she wanted to meet in our basement, where the boys were known to gather. She had some facts about alcohol she wanted us to know.

At this point, an intervention could have raised awareness and maybe brought change. But the meeting never happened. I was called to New Jersey to deal with the sudden death of my mom and heart surgery for my dad. I dropped the ball. My mind got diverted. Life went on as usual. I will always regret this!

When Matt turned sixteen, he bought his first car, a used black Honda. He found it on one of the Internet automobile websites. He and his dad went together to pick it up. Upon their return, I took the photo in the driveway of a proud father and son with the new shiny black Honda. It is so ironic and twisted to see now that my husband has his fingers crossed in this photo, but at the time it seemed cute.

We were proud of Matt being the designated driver as he was one of a few to own a car. We embraced a false sense of security, believing Matt was safe, thinking that he would not risk a DWI, thus losing his car and his license. There were drinking incidents the night of the junior prom. I was told that Matt, as designated driver, took a carload of friends home safely. I was proud that he was so responsible. But what about when he was not driving? Was he safe then? Did he focus more on not getting into trouble? One never thinks of the other alternative; death due to a drunken friend at the wheel. You don't think anything that horrific could happen. It was a false sense of security, thinking your son would be safe because he was the designated driver.

Marc was frustrated by the drinking. One night, he had a loud argument with Matt and took away his keys. Matt disappeared on his bike. We did not hear from him for hours. I was worried but exhausted from the conflict. I tried not to be frightened. At 2:00 a.m., we received a message on our recorder from Matt saying he was at the camp at Bloody Pond. He pedaled his bike for sixty miles in the dark, using a compass and a map! This was our strong-willed Matt, constantly trying both our patience and stamina.

In the spring of 2004, the drinking issues in our community became tragic. A young adult died after hitting a tree on a four-wheeler on his way home from a bar near his family's camp in the Adirondacks. Speed and alcohol were factors in the crash. Marc IV attended the funeral. He brought home beautiful photos of the family from a program at the service. I remember looking at the pictures and feeling sick. At dinner, I said to my children, "Please, just don't ever go too fast." Matt looked at me and said, "What are you talking about, Mom? I want to fly a jet!"

Another alcohol-related incident happened on the lake with boats. One evening, Marc IV left friends relaxing on their boat because he had to work the next morning. At home, he got a call that they were struck by another boat. A group of teens heading to a lakeside home crashed into them. Neither boat had its lights on. It was a small-town coincidence; brothers from the same family on each boat! It was a miracle that no one was hurt because kids from both boats were thrown out into the dark lake. One friend of Marc's said the oncoming boat missed his head by inches. This could have heightened community awareness, but few people ever found out about it. Because no one was hurt, no police report was filed.

The youth of Skaneateles were at risk. Families were in denial. We all were warned. Those of us who would never allow drinking in our homes only forced the kids out to fields and woods. Some looked the other way, in total denial. Some families let the kids drink in their homes, thinking it was a better way to keep them safe. The end result: a lot of drinking!

Later, in 2005 after Matt's death, Marc would open his statement in the courtroom with these words, "This sentence is a consequence of no consequences, of accepting unacceptable behavior regarding teenage drinking." Our vision of how we could have parented differently had become clearer to us. The way that society glorifies alcohol had become evident. We were seeing with new eyes. I would come to call this "fatal vision."

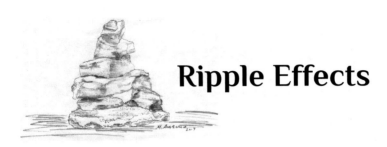

Ripple Effects

9/10/04

It's amazing how a few days can just bring you so low and sad. I am not feeling strong today. We have had a string of unbearable events and all has brought our pain to such an anguished level. I woke up after an anxious ridden night. It seemed almost as though it had just happened. I went to bed terribly lonely and depressed. Marc has not joined me the past few evenings and we have not connected at all lately.

The football game topped off an excruciating day for Marc and me. Not seeing Matthew on that field, not being a part of this team, not videotaping the National Anthem as my Matthew looked toward his country's flag made me cry sad tears. I cried lonely tears and wept for all of us.

The ripple effect of Matt's death was endless. People all over the country were reaching out to us. Letters poured in for weeks. I was shocked to see the mound of mail in the first few days. I had never witnessed anything like it.

I received letters from the Air Force cadets who supervised Matt in his one-week summer seminar. They were shocked and crushed that their leader of dodge ball and summer seminar academics was gone from this world. CIC Daniel L. Way had given him ten out of ten in all categories and written in his evaluation, "It would be an atrocity if Matthew Angelillo is not

a member of the AFA class of 2009. I have no doubt he will be a
model cadet and Air Force officer."

> Matt participated in all events and was motivated to
> learn about cadet life and the Academy. Matt was very
> motivated as a team player and his motivation rubbed off
> on all members of the team. Matt was the number one
> athlete of my element and arguably the best athlete of A
> flight. Matt encouraged others to follow my direction as
> well as set an incredible example of poise and confidence.
> Matt should be a member of the cadet wing.

> —Evaluation received from
> Daniel L. Way

Later that month, Matt would be posthumously appointed
to the Class of 2009. The burial at Lakeview Cemetery included
a folded flag given to me by Matt's Air Force mentor, Officer
Steve Hartnett. I can't describe the confusion in my heart as I
accepted it. We now display it in our family room in a frame built
by my brother.

One night in July, when we were gathered on our porch,
Matt's cell phone rang. Lindsay, having inherited Matt's phone,
ran to me in tears and said it was a friend of Matt's from the Air
Force. He was calling for Matt. I was stunned thinking about
what to say. I said, "I am so sorry to have to tell you this, but
Matthew is no longer with us. He was killed in a car crash last
week." How could these words come out of my mouth? This poor
kid was speechless. He said, "Oh my God, Matt and I talked
about rooming together! I wanted to go to Air Force with him!"

Another layer of sadness for friends we hadn't even met. A
few of these potential cadets wrote to me and expressed their
admiration for Matt. C1C Daniel L. Way wrote the following
to us:

> Matt stood out to me as an incredible young man. He had
> confidence and poise not common in young men his age.

I spent the most time with Matt during athletic events, especially dodge ball, where he excelled greatly. Matt was the number one athlete in my element and possibly the flight. He was always sure to include every member of the element. Matt's motivation and enthusiasm was very contagious and brought everyone's spirit up. Even though it was only a week, I felt close to your son because his personality was so warm and inviting. Matt was going to make an incredible cadet and professional Air Force officer. Indeed he had the right stuff.

—Daniel L. Way
USAF Academy

After the tragedy, we learned of people all over this country who were pulling for us. When I had a good day, I would call my sister, Susan, in New Jersey to tell her. She responded with, "That's what we all are praying for!"

We received a beautiful note from the very special priest who married us in 1981. Father John McDermott wrote, "Stay close to each other and look for every opportunity to point out goodness. Matthew wants you to do well as a family. He has bragged about all of you to everyone, so don't let him down. Work harder to be close to each other and to God, your friend."

Lynne Graci, my friend from Pennsylvania, wrote to me recalling special memories of Matt and her son, Paul, friends in nursery school.

Dear Marianne and Marc,

We send out love and heartfelt sympathy to you and your family. We have thought of little else since we heard the news of Matthew's death. We are heartbroken over the tragic loss of your Matthew.

I will always think of Matthew as the little boy I knew when we car-pooled to Great Beginnings Pre-School. What a pip! Was it a good Matthew day or a bad Matthew day? That was what the teacher asked when I dropped him off. He was already in charge. Did he want to go to school or was he just not in the mood that day. He was a beautiful boy with an already strong and determined personality.

I never had occasion to tell you how much I learned about being a mother from you Marianne. By the time we met you were already "Marc's mom" and had a world of experience compared to me. We met though the babysitting coop and I am thankful for that twist of fate. Your kids knew the joy of outside play and of entertaining themselves.

We talked about our two little neurotic boys and how they couldn't stand how certain things felt on their hands, wrist or neck. Buying clothes was a challenge. It was a little thing but I felt someone else understood how the seam of a shirt could send a kid over the edge. I will always remember "creek shoes", snakes, bugs, frogs, beautiful gardens, and paintings of beautiful gardens. I will always remember Matthew's incredible blue eyes and his boundless energy. It was clear at that early age that Matthew was incredibly bright and extremely charismatic.

My favorite memory of you has to do with food… peanut butter to be exact. You invited Paul and me over for lunch after pre-school one day. We chatted and went outside. I told you I needed to get lunch for Paul and you said they were having lunch already as you had put peanut butter, bread and butter knives out on the table. They were making their own sandwiches. Surprised I went back into the kitchen and found Paul puzzling over what *he* was supposed to do with peanut butter, bread and a knife. He had no idea what he should do with this momentous task. Okay, he was a sheltered guy. Matthew was happily eating his sandwich. Paul had no clue how to make a peanut butter sandwich. Oh well, the joy of an only child. I think maybe even Alex made his own sandwich that day. To this day I admire your determination to make the kids adept at doing things for themselves.

I have kept track of you and your family over the years and was always happy that you settled so quickly to your new home. There is never a day that I pass your Glendale Rd house without thinking of you. The silly broken fish fountain is still where you left it. The life of the house has never been the same.

I do not know how you feel. I do understand how much you loved your beautiful son. Will the hole in your heart and family ever heal? I believe you are strong enough to go on. I believe you are strong enough to make a great life for you and your other children. I believe in you. I believe in your love of your family.

For many months, I stayed close to home and visited with Matt's friends. His grave was a short walk from our home, and many of the friends would end up visiting his grave and sitting on our front porch. One by one they would seek me out. We called it having a "Matt moment." I would embrace their pain and encourage them to talk. They each wanted to share their stories of Matt and how much they missed him. Grief is such a strange emotion. So many do not know how to deal with it. You have the choice to run away from it or to embrace it by simply talking about it. I believe human nature often tempts us to avoid pain at all costs and to divert one's self so you don't think about it or feel it.

I first heard the term, "sharing my stones" from a friend at the Hope for Bereaved organization in Syracuse, New York. Jeanette explained the benefit of talking about your loved one. She explained sorrow was like holding a bag of heavy stones. If you share your pain, it is like giving out stones to others, and then your load you carry becomes lighter. I believe in this method of healing and have encouraged so many along the way to "share stones."

I have found that sharing grief and speaking about your loved one becomes easier over time. Even though it is difficult at first, eventually, you will find a way to think about your loved one with peace in your heart. It results in the ability to keep this person with you forever. As you reflect on your relationship with them, joy can come your way for having known them. Avoiding the pain and going around it usually results in the inability to let thoughts of this person come to mind. You end up losing them forever. This is the difficult choice one in grief must make.

There was one special friend of Matt's who I knew was hurting. My heart bled for Matt's girlfriend, Lauren. She was in a daze, crushed by the tragedy. She had a very special relationship with Matt and had looked forward to spending their senior year together. We asked her to just come along with us in whatever we did, spending time at our camp and evenings at our home. She seemed comforted by being around Matt's family. I would have done anything to ease her pain. She later wrote us a letter describing Matt's love for his friends and family. She wrote,

> I can't even explain how much of an impact Matt had on myself, my friends, and this whole community. He would do anything to make sure my friends, his friends, and myself were happy. Matt always worried about his friends and would get all stressed out when one of them was upset. He showed me love and I am so thankful.
>
> —Lauren Vitkus
> Class of 2005, Skaneateles

In the fall of 2004, I contacted a priest from a local church to meet with some of Matt's friends with whom he had received confirmation. I thought it would help them vent some of their emotions. I thought a priest could help encourage and deepen a belief in eternal life. One tends to not take these concepts seriously until you are face-to-face with the need for them. In all the healing I have read or learned about, expressing one's feelings is helpful. When you try to bury emotions, they get buried alive. But they still must be fed. And the food can be bitterness, resentment, and unhappiness.

These friends had suffered a traumatic experience, and I thought they could all benefit from talking. But they were in different places, their grief having different degrees. Each one of them had a unique relationship with Matt. The group met only a few times. The situation became even more difficult as they processed the conflict over supporting Steven and grieving for Matt. It was hard to do both at the same time. In addition, the complicated nature of Matt's death involving alcohol forced the grief even further deeper.

Dear Matt,

I'm supposed to be angry with you. Up until now I wasn't. But why shouldn't I be? You know you shouldn't have gotten into that car. I know you know it. You shouldn't have had so much to drink. Why? It was selfish. I know you weren't thinking that at the time. Clearly you weren't thinking at the time. But you had a choice. And don't think I don't believe you didn't know that was the wrong choice. You just thought it would be ok. Well guess what? It's not ok. You made one bad decision and look where it left us. All our town is a mess and how could you just leave? How could you not think about the consequences? Why did you think this time would be ok? It's just not fair. I know, life's not fair but especially this. And now no one will talk about you. No one will deal with your death. It's been swept under the rug and overshadowed because you were all drinking.

I know it wasn't your fault because you couldn't have known. But you should have. You left us all here, missing you terribly. And everyone does miss you. I wish there was a way for you to let us know you're all right. It's hard to just believe when everyone here is so not all right. I think it's important you know how many lives you've affected. And not just by dying. By living. Everybody liked you. Almost everybody anyway. You were just nice to people. There was this way about you made everyone feel as if they were really really special. I know you made me feel that way. It was always "Nance" thinking now that no one else called me that all the time. I don't think you ever once called me anything different. And you always wanted to work with me. I graded all your papers in English and we'd do "apush" assignments together. (Your research paper on Stephan Crane last year was by the way awful. I gave you a good grade anyway though.)

How could you be gone?

—Letter found in Nancy Menapace's journal
2004

It was a long difficult senior year for Matt's friends and my family. There is never a good time to lose a child, but I have to say that losing one before his senior year is an excruciating in-your-face loss. I still had two teenagers in school, and Alex was playing football. Just to walk near the football field or down the hall of the high school became unbearable. Seeing Matt's friends at a game or at the lake, going on as if life was normal, was extremely painful.

I remember telling the football coach I couldn't do the team's video or photography work. As I walked out that door, I felt as though my soul was crushed. How could this have happened? How could my number 29 be gone forever? At the end of the season, the coach presented us with a photo of a helmet and jersey lying on a bench with MA and #29 imprinted on it.

I still cannot believe how we got through this year with such strength despite our pain. I tried everything to reach out to Matt's class, to stay close to them. It helped to hug them, to see them, to talk to them. I needed to know that Matt was loved and missed. For me, any connection to his life was healing.

Journal Entry 8/24/04

Three of Matthew's girlfriends came to visit after a nice dinner party with the Kraus family. It was a joint grieving session as we remembered Matthew together. We talked and laughed about his idiosyncrasies, his messy book bag, messy locker with papers but how incredibly fast he was when it came to math problems. We all watched the slideshow and cried and missed him terribly. It was good to share my pain with these girls who loved him dearly. I had a lightened load for the next day and definitely felt better.

They asked me what helped my pain and I said "you." It is the truth. I would never want to scare any of these friends away with anger or disappointment because I need them desperately. They are the lifeblood to my son. They are his friends who he shared his life with. They knew him well and I want the connection to each one of them. They're sharing my pain and it's getting me through this.

At one point, I hosted a team dinner for the football team, serving Matt's favorite, pulled pork. Another night, Lindsay and I hosted Lauren with her friends for dinner. I tried to steer the conversation to Matt and how everyone was coping. Few of them could talk about it, Lauren no exception. Only years later would she share her pain with me.

That night, after dinner I went to my journal.

Journal Entry April 2005

I do miss the teenagers and the life they brought to my house. A friend of Lauren's confirmed what I already thought. Lauren suffers after she leaves our home. As much as I miss her, I truly do not want her to suffer. I want her to just remember Matt with love, not pain.

That fall, two of Matt's close friends were named co-captains of the football team that year. They were also the ones who had been charged with supplying the alcohol on the evening of the tragedy. There was publicity over their arrests, headlines, and front-page photos. One evening, they came to see Marc and me, distraught that the football coach had stripped them of their captainships. Wanting to be close to Matt's friends and support them, we tried to listen and be sympathetic. Marc explained to a local TV station, "These friends are like family to us, and we need to support them."

The grave became a place of mourning for many of us. I would find on it letters to Matt, flowers, lacrosse balls, hunting shells, and duck feathers. Teens set out solar lights so they could visit at night. One friend found me mourning one day, so we tried to comfort each other. He was with Matt on that last evening. He saw Matt get into the car. I cannot imagine the burden on these teens to relive that moment over and over.

Another difficulty was the placement of the grave. The Corsellos' house bordered the cemetery. It just happened that Steven's bedroom overlooked Matt's tombstone. This complicated trips to grieve because I did not feel that I had privacy. The *Post-Standard* included a photo of Steven overlooking the grave from his bedroom. Again, it was difficult for me to process Steven's pain along with my own...indescribable pain for all of us.

During this time of intense mourning, one of Matt's possessions became unbearable to see anymore: his black Honda. We asked Alex if he wanted it, and he said no. Marc and I could not handle the pain of seeing it in our driveway. At a family picnic, I mentioned it to my cousin, Joanne. Her son, who was Matt's age, was a special young man to all of us called the "miracle baby." My cousin had been in a car accident in her ninth month of carrying Nicholas. She had been on life support for weeks after Nicholas was safely delivered. Now, at the age of seventeen, Nicholas could drive. Joanne and her husband drove to Skaneateles one weekend during that painful summer and test-drove Matt's Honda to the lake. We sat at the waterfront and talked.

I saw Lauren and several of Matt's friends near us and thought of how painful that car had to be to them as well. All of a sudden, this group of teenagers ran to it and piled into it. I cried seeing grief-stricken teenagers processing something incredibly impossible. How could he be gone? Their suffering was real and painful, and there was nothing I could do. How could so many lives be so crushed by one missing person? I started thinking, *Why Matt? There were three boys in that car. Why our Matt?* I thought, *We had three sons and the other parents had only one. Did God not want to take away their only sons?*

Then I thought of Matt being the ringleader. Why would God take away the glue to this group? A friend of Matt's had told me, "If God asked all the teenagers for a volunteer to die for the rest of them, Matt would have volunteered."

One night, to an audience of DWI offenders, I asked that same question, "Why Matt?"

I followed it up with the only answer that made sense: "If Matt was chosen, then so was I. That's why I am here tonight to share our story. I want to be his voice."

> I never had someone who knew me as well as Matt did. He knew what I was thinking the majority of time and would be there for me. Whenever I had a problem, Matt was the first person I would call. He would help me in all ways possible. Whether it was school, friends, life, and even speeding tickets, I knew exactly who to call and was guaranteed the best advice.
>
> —Kevin Dale
> Class of 2005 Skaneateles

The pain of Matt's friends made my heart ache beyond belief. The friend who sat on Matt's lap in the two-seater Ferrari and was ejected from the vehicle, suffered enormously. He was confined to a couch with broken vertebrae and had to miss not only the funeral but also Matthew's wake and the entire summer of trying to heal emotionally with his friends. When I visited him, tears just fell from his eyes as he lay on the couch. His forced recuperation and complications from the crash, had isolated him from so many friends. One day after he was up and around again, he organized a breakfast at the local diner, the Cedar House, for Matt's friends and me. It was surreal, sitting at their regular hangout and hearing their conversations. I tried to picture how Matt fit into this group of lifelong friends and how he would have contributed to the conversations. I could just hear his sarcasm and playful bantering. I wanted to be Matt and help fill the hole.

Journal entry August 14th, 2004

> It was excruciating to see him grieve so. He questioned why God took Matt and not him. He remembered Steven's speed in the car and he asked him to slow down. He remembers nothing after the back end swerved out. He woke up in the emergency room overhearing there was a "dead on arrival" and thought of Steven first. He said Matthew could never die. He was too tough.

After breakfast, this friend asked me to go to the grave with him for his first time. There, he wept. He had been so sure Matt and he would be in each other's weddings. He couldn't imagine academic life without Matt to compete with because they had shared so many classes over their nine-year friendship. He explained how different everything was without Matt. He was the glue holding so many friendships together.

He and Matt had shared many years of memories. He was the driver of the four-wheeler when Matt broke his arm. He was with Matt for hockey, touch football, and the gatherings in our basement. Their friendship was deep, and he would be forever changed by the tragedy.

I had used Matt's prom photo to have Mass cards made. I laminated them so they could be displayed in rooms, on dashboards, in wallets. Kevin's dad was worried about his son, as were the other parents, because he would find his son in bed, holding the card and crying. It was heart wrenching. If I could have brought Matt back just for them, I would have.

As time went by and the reality hit us, the pain became intimidating. Many of Matt's friends could not bear to see our hurt. As people went back to their regular lives, our lives became more difficult. We missed Matt more every day, and the shock started to transition from disbelief to the excruciating acceptance that we would never see our son again.

Coping

9/28/04

Here I sit at the point on an incredibly beautiful day. It's been a string of nice days in September and I have been grateful for this peace in my life. I can hear life calling me back in to resume my hectic schedule and something in me craves this absolute peace. I have been stealing hours everyday not caring what is left behind. The phone, jobs, people and my computer are all calling for me. I have little stamina to forge on. I get worn down by small talk and need in a big way to be with anyone representing some bit of healing.

My family coped as best we could. We surrounded ourselves with loved ones and friends, and they carried us through the first year. We were rarely without a dinner invitation or family function to attend. My nephews spent many weekends with us that summer. We continued to fish and go to our camp in Marathon, and I just don't know how we did it…but we did.

I remember reading book after book about grief and healing, trying to stay sane. The best advice: stay in the present; don't wander into the past or future. Both were too painful to ponder. I tried to plan simple pleasurable moments. I learned that more good can be done over a cup of coffee with a friend than anything else. My friend, Dale, spent hours with me on a bench that we claimed as our own on Skaneateles Lake.

Journal Entry May 2nd, 2005

My greatest gift is my friend, Dale, this winter. We spent endless hours discussing our pain, disappointment, anger, hopes and dreams. She shared all with me, and we crashed right though the center of grief together. I have loved her deeply and appreciate all the times she picked me up with my dog, Mavis, and went to find a spot to talk, usually a bench in the park by Skaneateles Lake. I wish I could help her beyond listening but I don't have the energy to do much else. I pray I do not become selfish if I am not already.

That first year, I spent so much time with people that I worried that I would wear out the friends and family in my life. They were always listening, always concerned and sympathetic. My goal was to find some positive in this horrific situation. I wrote and read and shared endlessly. Somehow, writing it down seemed to help me sort it out.

Journal Entry July 3rd, 2004

Love continues to get me through the day—lots of it. I still have so much pain being alone. I need lots of people, lots of love, and especially the presence of Matthew's life around me.

It's a rollercoaster of emotions. Some moments are numbing and tolerable. People continue to move me through my day. Food still arrives; companionship helps; love is available any minute of the day. I am one phone call away from healing and friendship.

We've grieved again and again. I miss Matthew terribly and miss my bright shining star. The letters continue to arrive which bless his love and energy for life. I am so completely proud of him and wanted nothing more than to follow his success. Now I am reduced to wallowing in it because it will always be tainted with disappointment.

I am praying for strength to get through the days. I don't want to know the events of that dark night, but I have to recognize his calling for something bigger and better. So many people have written to say their life has been altered, improved, or touched in some way. I pray each day improves all of us.

I will cherish my memories of Matthew, which I have created via camera each day the past seventeen years. I love his smile, his wit, and even appreciate his temperament which I understand a bit more after these past two weeks. He devoted himself to everyone around him. He shared more than we ever imagined. He cared more than we ever knew. As Marc said so beautifully in the funeral program, "He made a difference."

In a period of profound strength during 2005, Marc wrote a hopeful piece called "The Tragedies of Life," which was published in the Syracuse *Post-Standard*.[2] He writes,

"You must prepare yourself for the tragedies of life,…" these words were spoken to me by Lou Griesenback, a close friend and mentor a few weeks prior to my wedding in 1981. His words of advice came in a discussion after his adult son, daughter-in-law, and grandson were tragically killed in a house fire in Montclair, New Jersey.

Those words have caused curiosity in me for years since hearing them as a young adult setting forth to create a new life and family with my soon to be wife, Marianne. What exactly did he mean by a 'tragedy of life'? Back in 1981 I had recently graduated from college, was beginning a career and would soon be married. My stable childhood did not include growing up with divorced parents, death of any family members, terminal illness or the experience of grief. Tragedies to me were not really tragedies at all but disappointments. Failing to make a starting team, a poor grade in class, rejection from a friend or potential employer were the only 'tragedies' I had experienced. How was I to comprehend the depth of grief he was experiencing when he spoke those words? I clearly lacked the life experiences he had as a sixty-seven year-old man.

On Fathers Day, June 20, 2004, life granted me the opportunity to walk in his shoes. My teenage son, Matthew, was a victim of a fatal automobile accident. The late night telephone call that all parents fear came. The words of the county sheriff, "Are you the father of Matthew Angelillo? There has been an accident and I'm sorry, your son did not survive."

The task of informing my wife, his mother, she has lost a son. The calls to family members that were necessary and so difficult to make. This was the beginning of my new life and identity. For the first time in my life, a true tragedy had occurred. The wave of grief sets in like a terminal illness. It isn't as bad as you can imagine, it's much worse. It is unrelenting and paralyzing. It causes physical pain and mental anguish. 'Life altering,' is a term that best describes an experience of this magnitude. The statement I had heard twenty-three years ago now became a question I needed to answer, "Was I prepared?"

Prior to Matt's accident, I couldn't define the term grief. Several years before, I had lost my father, whom I loved dearly. I viewed the experience as part of life. He was loved by many, gave my mom and five siblings a wonderful life, and enjoyed the blessing of eleven grandchildren. I remember telling my wife, who still had both parents, that it was nothing you could prepare yourself for. Death is so final. Holidays would be different, the first birthday card I received after his death read, "Love, Mom." These were all reminders of his absence. The grief came and went. But, I had my children to raise. That too was part of life, my life.

Preparing yourself for the "tragedies of life" isn't the same as getting ready for a trip, where everything can be done in the final hours. It is a way of life, a life of responsibility, generosity and kindness. It is developing and nurturing relationships along the way, realizing that everyday I might meet someone that will change my life forever. It's a life of optimism and accepting fate, believing that something good can really come from all of life's challenges. It is believing in spiritual intervention, the healing power of nature, and realizing that it doesn't matter what we expect from life, rather it's about what life expects from us.

Dr. Viktor Frankl, author-psychiatrist, survivor of concentration camps in Auschwitz and Dachau, wrote in *'Mans Search for Meaning'*, "If there is meaning in life at all, then there must be meaning in suffering. Suffering is an ineradicable part of life, even as fate and death. Without suffering and death, human life cannot be complete."

Accepting my fate as a father, who has lost a son, represents my suffering. Was I prepared for a tragedy as great as losing a child? Absolutely not, but I am prepared to go on living. Life will forever be changed, but it doesn't have to be bad. I have an obligation to comfort those who are suffering with me, and to give hope to those who will undoubtedly experience similar loss. Life is worth living, only now with a greater sensitivity and purpose.

—Marc C. Angelillo
February 20, 2005

Everyone's grief journey is different. Mine certainly was a bit unique, with so much of my life immersed in photography and video. I surrounded myself with photos and videos of Matt. I put my favorite clips on a hard drive, and I would absorb his face and smile. In my own crazy way, I spent hours keeping him alive in my mind and my soul. If anyone dared to ask, I was willing to share. I healed through these images, and I am so incredibly grateful to have them. I looked through hours of old footage, saving memories as if I had uncovered a treasure. This became a part of my healing journey.

Nature and the outdoors helped our moods. Despite the pain, we decided to follow through with a planned camping trip to

Lake George. It had been our annual vacation, sharing an island with fellow outdoor enthusiasts and friends. It was one of our favorite places, and I loved waking up to a majestic lake view from our tent. We were close with a few families and their children. We would boat our camping gear to a campsite on an island. There, we would laugh, swim, bathe, bond, and eat together for a few memorable days. Our children loved this vacation, and so we decided to try it without our beloved Matt.

August 1st, 2004 Camping on Lake George

We had a beautiful morning on a Lake George point watching the sun breaking through clouds. My spirits are lifted in an amazing way. I enjoy everything about this spot. The friendships are perfect, the children are wonderful to watch and observe, the scenery is completely tranquil, and our basic needs are all taken care of. Food, warmth, companionship, and visual beauty are wrapped into one. Yes, this vacation has been the most healing of the last six weeks.

Maureen and Marty have been great empathetic listeners; Pete and Beth have provided the laughter and diversion needed. I am thankful to have had these days and now don't want to move on—once again. We get settled into some comfort and support, only to have to try again in the painful atmosphere called our home.

It's so painful missing Matthew in our home especially. I visit the room shared by him and Alex, see all his math and chemistry by his bed, touch his clothes and green down comforter he wrapped himself in for the past eight years. I see his photo of him and his friends over his desk. I sit in his chair he used hour after hour each school evening. I am ripped apart. Yet I can love summer so much here in Lake George on this island. I am amazed that God can create a heart which loves and cries so hard and which can experience joy and pain in such a deep traumatic way. Never have I felt such a tearing in my heart and soul. I want to talk to Matt so badly. I want to envision him with a life better than the one we had prepared for him here. God help me, and Matthew bless me. Especially bless your broken-hearted father.

Again, nothing can soothe the heart more than nature and especially the majestic hills and farms surrounding Skaneateles. Two of my good friends chipped in and bought me a bike so I could join them on the many beautiful roads of Central New York. Biking would be a huge source of comfort, beauty, and healing for me for years to come.

The holidays were another issue. One helpful thing I recently recommended to a fellow grieving mother was to change everything up. We tried to alter a few traditions and make them appear different—just to mask the hole in our lives. Christmas felt completely different. We hosted Marc's sister and young family instead of taking the traditional New Jersey road trip. We watched these beautiful, excited, young children open their gifts; and we could feel the joy of such a warm, loving family. It helped to make Christmas different. Our expectations were not the same.

When your child is gone, another date that looms with distress is the birthday. For us, each January 20 triggers sorrow and heartache.

We made it through Matt's eighteenth birthday starting with a beautiful memorial celebration at St. Mary's. The day began well, no tears. Father McGrath said a touching mass, speaking to each of us personally. His main message to the teens: "You have so much potential! Go out there and do God's will."

It was a powerful moment, as we reflected on our loss and how it had changed so much for so many. Life is different, as are our hopes and dreams. Our perspective on this life versus eternal life is more prevalent. This life is precious, but it's over so quickly. We have such a brief opportunity to make our mark. However, our "mark" can be a series of small ones. Many may seem insignificant, but they can add up.

Journal Entry 1/20/05

I had such a happy day on January 20th. Friends, family and Matt's friends surrounded me. It was wonderful having Matt's friends spend so much time with me. We reached and overcame a major hurdle of pain, guilt and anger. We needed to gather to celebrate Matt's life and commemorate his passions and unique personality traits. We laughed over old pranks, photos, video clips of thirteenth and fourteenth birthday parties and the junior prom. I made sure Lauren was all right with it. We enjoyed seeing his personality jump out, his smile and all his mannerisms. We miss you so much Matt. I came away on your birthday filled with love and friendship and hope for our meeting again in eternal life.

Many people carried us through that first year. Dale contacted a Syracuse organization called Hope for Bereaved, and she asked what she could do to help. A few weeks after the funeral, she organized a morning coffee with the head of the organization, Therese Schoeneck, who had lost a child twenty years ago in a similar crash. I remember asking, "Will this pain ever stop?" Therese reassured me that it does soften over time, that there is definitely "hope for the bereaved."

It meant a lot to speak with someone who had walked in my shoes. She looked *normal* and appeared content and purposeful, which gave me hope for my family and me. She said, "You will never be the same, but you can be a good new you." Therese also told me that the best thing I could do for my family was to work on healing myself.

Some friends could not understand what had happened to us. A few wanted to know if I would ever be "normal" again. Two weeks after the crash, one told my husband, "Move on." Another told me, "You must focus on the living and not be obsessed with Matt." I couldn't get Matt out of my mind. I thought about him constantly.

I read a book called *Lament for a Son* by Nicholas Wolterstorff.³ The author wrote about why he needed to think about his deceased son more than his living children: "Because he's the only one with a grave."

So that became my excuse, my reason why Matt was such a fixture in my mind. Matt needed to be represented to make up for his physical absence. Recently, I helped a bereaved mother after her daughter's sudden death. I explained how a sudden death is so different from one from natural causes or a prolonged illness. The shock lasts so long. It takes enormous energy to process what has happened. We can never be prepared for having a happy family one day and the next day be experiencing utter despair. You just can't get your mind around the loss. The suffering is unbearable. Each morning, you wake up to the nightmare, remembering it all over again and wondering if it's real or not. "Matt is dead?"

One bereaved mother told me she used to love gardening, but now she can't even look at her flowers. I told her, "Your mornings may never be the same." Sunrises, garden walks, coffee moments—the simple things we take for granted can become tainted for a very long time. As the country singer, Kenny Chesney, says in a song called, "Who'd You'd Be Today," "Sunny days seem to hurt the most." It's the realization that the sun used to be able to fix anything—but not anymore. All your problems and bad moods used to be alleviated by a sunny day. After the death of a child, it merely brings the realization that everyone else is happy—but you.

I told one recently bereaved mother that long ago, a woman wore black for a year to let everyone know she was grieving. People would know not to expect anything from her. The black would tell others that a heart was broken and that they should be treated with the utmost care. Nowadays, our society expects one to pick up immediately and just "get over it and focus on the living."

Jerry Sittser's *A Grace Disguised* would become a bible of grief for me. This was the first grief book put into our hands. Sittser lost his wife, mother, and young daughter in a car crash. He describes his suffering so powerfully yet also gives hope when he writes,

> The accident remains now, as it always has been, a horrible experience that did great damage to us and to so many others. It was and will remain a very bad chapter. But the whole of my life is becoming what appears to be a very good book.[4]
>
> —Jerry Sittser
> *A Grace Disguised*

Sittser encourages others by stressing that the sorrowful soul can grow from loss. He encourages the bereaved, saying, "To achieve transformation, you have to let go of regrets over what could have been and pursue what can be."

I believe this is the most difficult part of grief in the first years. One must process the utter despair they feel from the disappointment over what could have been. Matt had such hope and promise; he was such a unique individual, and he was destined for accomplishing such incredible things. From being a sensitive caring friend and sibling to a competitive athlete and a gifted student with amazing energy, Matt was someone I wanted to follow my whole life. Not only was he my son, but he was going to always be a part of my future, surprising me with his intellect, sensitivity, and energy. The astounding disappointment is so difficult to process. Nothing will ever be the same without Matt.

Fatal Vision

Journal Entry 2005

I am mad at Matt today. I am disappointed that he chose to risk everything. I am mad he forgot all his senses, his recognition of right from wrong. I am mad about his temporary lapse of concern for himself, for us, for Lauren, for all who loved him. I cannot fully absorb our loss and pain. I cannot fully absorb all the terrible pain these students have caused us. I say these students but I mean everyone, all those who taught these teens the passion for fun, excitement, danger, sports cars, going fast, and the desire to drink, laugh, and be social. I blame all of us here today and always.

I had no idea that opinions about a drunk teenage driver causing a fatality would be debated by an entire community for months and that friendships would be forever tainted. I never knew death could be become so complicated. If one dies by an act of God, such as disease or an accident, the acceptance of death may be easier because nothing you could have done would have prevented it. But society understands that a crash caused by a drunk driver is "no accident." It is avoidable and punishable. By law, it is vehicular manslaughter regardless of the driver's age. Within the year, Matt's friend, Steven, would be charged with three felonies.

It is difficult to describe the insanity of those days leading up to a sentencing. Some friends pulled me aside to say I had to keep Steven out of prison. They said it was wrong to put a teenager in prison. "It was an accident!" they said, and I would not want Matt imprisoned if the roles were reversed.

I was in so much pain. I could not handle taking on Steven's consequences or lack thereof. I wanted it to be totally in the hands of the court. Marc went to the judge and let it be known that he did not need to put Steven in prison for us. No punishment would be worthy of our son's life. Our family did not require a prison sentence.

I was reminded of an accident in New Jersey where a teen killed his younger cousin in a drunk-driving crash. The family of the victim never pressed charges, and the driver walked free. But later, the driver suffered from drinking problems despite the lack of punishment. Hearing that story, I felt angry because I felt that if the driver had suffered some consequence years ago, perhaps it could have made a difference across the country, and maybe my son would be alive. Perhaps stiffer consequences for DWI could prevent more tragedies.

For days, the press hounded us. Early on, I was contacted by Hart Seely, a reporter for the Syracuse daily paper. He said he desperately wanted to write an article for a three-day series in the *Post-Standard*. I remember seeing him standing on my front porch, and the crushing despair made me close the door and say no. It was just too overwhelming and too painful.

A few weeks later, I received a letter from Hart, asking me to reconsider. He said boldly, "I must write this story. And the reason is simple. I have three children, ages sixteen, thirteen, and ten. I am writing it for them." His letter made me realize that this tragedy was not just about Steven and Matt. There was a grander scale to consider.

I decided to support Hart, but I had to protect my heart. Eventually, I called him and said, "Please come over and you are welcome to get to know Matt by going through Matt's memory books." I will never forget seeing Hart at my kitchen table with tears in his eyes as he read Matt's letters. I asked him later, as we got to know each other well, "Hart, what came first, the heart or the name?" Definitely, this reporter was the right one for this very difficult story. He brought sensitivity, objectivity, and compassion for all involved.

Hart interviewed many people in Skaneateles. He poured his heart and soul into this story. He interviewed Steven, Jules, Skaneateles law enforcement, an administrator at the church, assorted parents of teenagers over the years, and me. He clearly and poignantly documented the devastation to our community. He also accurately portrayed the alcohol problem and concerns in the community leading up to this tragedy. This three-part series, headlined "Kids drink, someone dies—a Central New York community discovers the real painful cost of drunk driving," was published just prior to Steven's sentencing in March 2005. It later was reprinted for schools as a stand-alone educational article with the front page explaining the need for such an in-depth look at a tragedy.[5]

> You can read statistics and go numb with numbers. No matter how compelling the facts they represent, they don't always get to the heart and soul of the matter.
>
> Statistics on young drivers who drink and die, or cause death for others, are disturbing and cry out for attention. But numbers are abstract, and don't tally up the human loss in a way that might truly lead someone to change.
>
> Staff writer, Hart Seely of the *Post-Standard* spent months meeting with family and community members, trying to take the measure of the human loss behind one of those statistics. It is the story of one death, one arrest and future imprisonment, one community. But it speaks profoundly to the human loss in every one of those statistics: loss of life, loss of freedom, loss of a sense of security for an entire community.

The more those statistics take on flesh and bones and the faces of real people, the more we feel what is lost when this happens. Perhaps raising awareness in our community about the true cost of drinking and driving will lead all of us to do what we must to prevent it.

In that spirit, we reprint this series that first appeared in the *Post-Standard* March 6, 7, and 8, 2005

—*Post-Standard*, 2005

I have handed out this series to many students over the years. It still reduces me to tears. I thank the *Post-Standard* for its vigilance in making these tragedies public. I thank Hart for helping to share Matt's story, and I know his own children have benefited from it to this day. He remains one of my very close friends.

It was extremely difficult for my family to be so public, but I accepted the challenge to increase awareness and bring about change. In the meantime, more teenagers were losing their lives.

Journal entry
2005

I have sent the book, *A Grace Disguised* to another poor parent of a victim to drunken driving. A sixteen-year-old was killed by her best friend in a DWI the other night. It made me angry all over again, and I experienced the anger my family and friends felt when they read about Matthew's tragedy. I now feel the anger and senselessness of it all from an onlooker's perspective.

Within months of our tragedy, a close family friend received a phone call that her daughter at Penn State University had been found hypothermic, lying on a street corner in the early morning outside a fraternity house. She had survived some horrific fall. No witnesses had come forward. She had been rushed to an emergency room with injuries that included a collapsed pelvis. She only remembered passing out in the fraternity house after a few drinks. Authorities brought no charges and discovered no explanation for her injuries. In the end, it was just another alcohol-related incident on a college campus.

Statistics paint a frightening picture of binge drinking on college campuses. In 1999, Harvard University's School of Public Health College Alcohol Study surveyed students at 119 colleges.[6] Here are some of the findings:

> A higher percentage of binge drinkers than non-binge drinkers reported having experienced alcohol-related problems since the beginning of the school year. Frequent binge drinkers were 21 *times more likely* than non-binge drinkers to have:

> - ⼈ Missed class
> - ⼈ Fallen behind in school work
> - ⼈ Damaged property
> - ⼈ Been hurt or injured

We watched our friends suffer through their daughter's difficult rehab period, but they were grateful to have her alive. They did not have to walk in our shoes. So again, I wondered, *Why Matt? Why was our son not so lucky? And who would be next to fall from a night of drinking or drugs?* My sister, Susan, often wonders, when hearing of tragic accidents, *Did alcohol play a role?*

I was becoming vocal in the community about teen drinking. In the year after Matt's tragedy, other drunk-driving accidents occurred. The Syracuse community was outraged and worried about the decisions being made by teens. I called a local radio station, *The Jim Reith Show*, and publicly invited any teenager into our home to see for himself or herself the suffering that my family was experiencing. I said, "When you drink, you don't think. All the rules and good character traits you have learned all your life go out the window with one evening of risk taking. I will share my pain if it saves a life." I then wrote a letter to the *Post-Standard*. It was titled, "It Didn't Work."[7]

It Didn't Work

My husband and I have not been ignorant regarding teenage drinking. We thought we would be successful following many of Dr. Welch's suggestions. We allowed an occasional glass of wine at holiday dinners, a spiked Shirley Temple at a family wedding under our supervision and have held ourselves to responsible drinking. We have kept lines of communication open with our teenagers and stressed the dangers of drinking and driving. Requiring our children to work for their cars assured us that they would never risk losing their cars or licenses to irresponsible driving. Drinking and driving was zero tolerance.

Recognizing that teenage drinking will occur anyway and therefore following the suggestion to "just make sure they call for a ride home no questions asked" does not work. I dare any parent to try it and pray for a safe outcome. The problem with any drinking at all is that all the rules, good character traits, and good judgment you have bestowed on your children for years goes out the window when they are under the influence of anything (alcohol or other drugs). They are caught up in the party, in the moment, and do not want any adult to intervene. Rarely will a call be made to a parent in this situation, especially if it is at a location not allowed (home of another student, or field). The resulting situation is cars full of teenagers with limited designated drivers available to get everyone home safely. The few students who abstained are responsible for everyone and cannot handle the situation themselves. Did they call a parent in our situation? No...Fear was a factor for some, and impaired judgment for others.

The only message to sound loud and clear is fear, pain and more pain. I commend the *Post-Standard* for putting this in everyone's face everyday and sending the message home consistently. I invite any teenager or parent into my home to witness the intolerable grief over losing a child tragically to a drinking and driving incident...I will share my pain if it saves a life.

I also challenge parents today to take the hard road and start active participation. This means making a few important phone calls to authorities when they come upon teenage drinking or drugs. Yes, this means not looking the other way. Perhaps this also means that their children may be under the athletic code and could be required to miss a few "important games"…Trust me…the pain you and your child will endure will be far less than ours.

So, what do we do? Let's start with finding some responsible teenagers out there to lead by example. There has to be some in every class who can be utilized to mentor others and clearly demonstrate that fun can be had without alcohol…Also, if they have goals and dreams…. assure them how easy all the dreams in the world will be lost with one second of bad judgment. Let's keep talking.…

—Marianne Angelillo
Mother of Matthew
Post-Standard Letter

This was the beginning of my stand, of my outrage over underage drinking. It was difficult. Friends called me "judgmental." One pulled me aside to say I was losing friends. My husband and I took the criticism hard. We wanted to protect others from experiencing our pain and suffering, but some did not see our true intentions. It was not about judging people. It was about wanting the world to be a better place. We wanted to stop the deaths, to stop the insanity, and give purpose to Matt's life and death.

I spoke first at Cayuga County Drug and Alcohol prevention night. I prepared a video about Matt's life. I poured over clips of Matt, fishing, hunting, on prom night, and in lacrosse games. He would be hiding behind bushes from my camera, shooting ducks, playing basketball with his brothers, and laughing with friends. This was the son we lost.

The talk went well. A few tears were shed. I was asked again to speak at schools, for driver education, and parenting programs.

Speaking became a part of my healing process. A local TV anchorman once asked me, "Do you think the kids are listening?"

I believed that if I could touch just one, then it was worth my effort. But I think the most powerful part of my presentation was not the tragedy but Matt's life and what we lost. The images of him *living* are what touched the students. The loss hit people hard. As later *Post-Standard* articles noted, the faces behind the tragedies are what will impact people the most.

In 2006, I was asked to do an interview for a show called *License to Live*. I accepted but, at the last minute, felt overwhelmed and fearfully under-confident to go on the show. I called my sister to discuss my concerns. She told me to pray on it, and the words would come. I decided to keep the appointment. Dan Cummings, a well-known anchorman in Syracuse, was to host the show. The interview brought out feelings I never anticipated. I was asked, was Matt a risk taker? Yes, Matt would leap off high cliffs into water or hit huge jumps on his snowboard, but I was sure of one thing: my son did not want to die on the evening of June 20, 2004. He had big plans and lofty goals. He had no idea that his life would only last seventeen years. Matt would be shocked to find he would be gone before his senior year of high school. Matt did not want to leave this world. A friend confirmed this for me by telling me about a conversation with Matt after he was driving home from skiing one night. Matt hit an icy patch in the road, and the car skidded into a 360 turn, stopping on the shoulder. He told a friend he thanked God it wasn't his time. He had too much to live for.

The second year after Matt's death, Marc and I scrutinized what we could have done as parents to prevent it. The teen drinking that had been curtailed in Skaneateles after Matt's death was resuming. There were many incidents, and our daughter, Lindsay, who was now in high school, showed many similarities to Matthew's personality. I decided to join a parenting organization called PACT—for parents, teens, and community together. PACT was created by Matt's hockey coach and wife after the tragedy. Chuck and Pat Gridley knew the timing was right to attract over one hundred people to an initial meeting. They sought to launch conversations between parents, teens, and the schools.

Marc and I attended a meeting, which turned out to be extremely difficult. Speaking out on underage drinking requires you to share hard realities about what you did wrong as parents. Marc shared some of our experiences, and it was painful. We also realized what we were speaking out against—that *rite of passage.*

PACT focused on the high school athletic code, making sure it was enforced and taken seriously. We noticed an improvement in the athletes' commitment to not drink during the sports season. This gave parents comfort as a three-sport athlete could be safe for most of the school year. We also realized that it is up to parents to be vigilant about drinking opportunities. Many stopped allowing drinking in their homes and would even call others to make sure an event would include a parent to supervise.

The parents of Lindsay's class started to turn the tide. Marc and I stayed home many evenings while teens gathered at our home. We hosted an after-the-junior-prom sleepover, patrolling tents all night. Another parent hosted a few parties, checking book bags and being vocal about her intolerance of underage drinking. I saw things improve. It took parenting education and the death of my son to start to change Skaneateles. *Matt, were you our sacrifice? I am so sorry it had to be you and us.*

I found this journal entry recently and thought how much Matt's death gave us such a different vision. We changed so much from those parents we were in 2002 when Marc IV was eighteen and Matt was fifteen.

January 1, 2002

We had a wonderful dinner last night with all of our friends celebrating the New Year. It was such a beautiful setting complete with fireworks over the lake. We came home to a "ripper" at our house, with bags of beer cans everywhere. Marc and his friends had taken over for a while. Matt and his friends did a good job keeping up. This morning there were bodies in the family room spread all over so I am hiding in the living room.

Through PACT, Marc and I spoke for the first time in Skaneateles. This was difficult because it's always easier to leave your community and address strangers. Seeing friends and neighbors in the audience was challenging as was accepting those who did not come.

The evening became a night of sharing by parents and teachers of children who had suffered from drugs or alcohol. Having a chance to impart our "fatal vision" helped us heal. Marc was amazing that night, challenging students and parents to make a contract to not drink and drive. Marc said to parents, "Tell your student, I won't 'drink and drive' if you don't."

A parent called later that night to say his son, leaving the event, suggested such a contract. Our children want to see parents be as safe and responsible as we ask them to be. How can we ask children to not drink and drive if we do it?

Marc sent a letter into the editor called "It's Up to Us."[8]

My wife, Marianne, and I, are acutely aware of every DWI tragedy that occurs in our area. They are not accidents. We used to grieve for the victims, now our thoughts go immediately to the parents, and family left behind. There is no greater loss in this world than losing a child. Grief is a debilitating condition that is unrelenting and life altering. Think for just one minute of never seeing your son or daughter again in this life, you will now understand the level of anxiety a grieving parent lives with the remaining 1,439 minutes per day.

For eighteen months, I have reflected on every way my son's death could have been avoided, and every other DWI victim that lost their life so unnecessarily. Where did we as parents go wrong? We discussed the dangers of drinking and driving constantly. The consequences, if our children were caught drinking, were firmly established. We cited every tragedy that has occurred and made them aware of them. Matt and Steven attended classes on DWI prevention. It obviously didn't work. As my wife, Marianne, has stated, "When you drink, you don't think."

The problem is that our society glorifies the use of alcohol in many aspects of our life. Entertainment, social gatherings, celebrations—the list of alcoholic events is endless. The beer and liquor industries have accomplished their goals of having alcoholic beverages standard at ball games, family picnics, car races, and graduations. They have led us to drink, but they do not pour it down our throats. Free will and peer pressure accomplish that.

Since I lost my son, I have made a conscious effort to abstain from drinking socially. I can tell you first hand, it is difficult. Initially, family and friends were not prepared to offer anything when I visited except alcoholic beverages, but that has now changed. It is sometimes uncomfortable, but I do not waver. I ask myself, "What good has ever come from drinking?" The answer is always the same—nothing.

My point is this. When you drive you must not drink, period. This is the answer to ending DWI tragedies. I regret ever attending a family picnic, or social gathering with my children, having a couple of beers throughout the event, and driving my family home. Was I drunk? I believe not. What I did accomplish was to set an example that driving and drinking was acceptable, as long as I wasn't drunk. This is the way parents and kids think today. The person who drinks the least is the designated driver.

Back in the sixties, our country had a problem with littering. There were numerous commercials that exposed the problem. Do you remember the crying Native American looking at a littered landscape? Our country, for the most part, became aware of the problem and it is now unacceptable to litter. My children would be appalled if we were to roll down the window of a vehicle and toss away garbage. That is how drinking and driving should be viewed. It starts at home, and it should start early. We set the example for our kids in everything we do, or don't do. Parents, stop drinking when you are expected to drive. This is the right thing to do—always.

—Marc C. Angelillo
Skaneateles, New York
1/11/06

Our tragedy had thrust us into the newspaper, radio, TV, and now into schools. Going public meant upping the ante in our lives. Grief could be mixed with the complexities of wanting societal change. This complicated our healing process.

One Boy Goes
to Prison

Journal Entry
March 1st, 2005

I told the Corsellos in my recent visit, that we are on the same side. We are the victims of a town's problems. All the teenage drinking going on forever and we hold the pain for all. I feel bad for Steven's Dad. He tried so hard to fight alcohol in this town including abstaining himself. He failed and we all failed.

The day after Matt died, Marc and I marched down the street to Steven's home and asked him to make something of his life in Matt's memory. We would forgive him.

It was the first time we'd seen Steven since the crash. We knew few details about the tragedy. We knew he had been driving the Ferrari at an incredibly excessive speed. The details were unclear, but we knew Steven never wanted to harm his friends. Marc and I hugged him. It was surreal how much his frame matched Matt's and to know Matt was not there to be hugged anymore.

Months later, Steven Corsello pleaded guilty in Onondaga County Criminal Court to charges of vehicular homicide, driving while intoxicated, and vehicular assault. The court set a sentencing date of June 2005, which would let Steven finish his senior year at Skaneateles. We occasionally spent time with Steven, waiting for his sentencing. We tried to include him in gatherings of friends at our home. I hugged Steven often. I tried to make him feel forgiven and welcome. One day, Matt's friends came to help Marc install a new window in my bedroom. Steven came too, and we looked at each other—deeply—for a long time.

Journal Entry-October 2004

> He said how sorry he was with his eyes. I felt it and I felt compassion for him in my heart. I did not feel any anger; I felt such sadness and regret. He does not know what words to say. I honestly feel different. I feel compassion and a friendly love. He was my son's good friend for a long time. I told him it would get better for all of us. He will survive this. He can be a better person. I gave him a copy of a *Purpose Driven Life* and I hope it can help him. I saw real feelings today—not shock or numbness or a shell. I saw the real Steven and his eyes were sorry. I am too.

I tried to hide my pain from Steven, but as the news coverage and the investigation dragged on, our relationship became strained. It grew more difficult, more painful. I had a hard time handling criticisms of the public. For me, the issue had become a lesson for teens, not punishing Steven or protecting him from it. I wanted to turn it over to the courts rather than have my heart make the decisions. I was in too much pain. I did not want to be responsible for the outcome. I ached with the need to know that Matt did not die in vain. Society had to understand the pain and devastation. This death was preventable and unnecessary. Our suffering needed some purpose and meaning.

April 8th, 2005

> Steven came over this afternoon and we had such an emotional conversation. He wanted us to know that it was because of us he survived this whole ordeal. Wow. Marc and I thanked him again for pleading guilty and avoiding a trial. He said Matt would always say, "take it like a man." He thought of Matt—"that's what Matt would have done."

In the spring of 2005, Steven's sentencing neared. On the day before his day in court, Steven's mother Nan came to see me. We sat on my porch, and she asked me to go to the judge and ask that Steven be spared prison. I was stunned. The day before, Steven had come to tell us he accepted his fate and was prepared to serve prison time. He said he felt it would help him heal in the right way. I told Nan I believed the court had to make the final decision. I could not interfere this late in the process. My broken heart could not take on the Corsellos' pain. I was not capable of going to battle for Steven. I wanted Steven to serve some type of punishment, decided by a judge—not me. I was not capable of making a decision. I could not get my mind around Steven's fate.

June 24th 2005

> Steven came over this week and I could see he came to talk. We had a true heart to heart and he needed to tell me what he was thinking. He gave me his apology that he would be reading in court. He told me he was not dreading Wednesday, the day of sentencing. He said the pain of prison was far surpassed by the pain of losing Matt. He reaffirmed his friendship with Matthew and said he thinks of him always. He said he doesn't do anything without thinking of our family first. He said he wanted me to take care of me—and not worry about him. He said how much Marc and I have helped him and each time he comes down to see us, he feels better when he leaves. I asked him if he was angry at Matthew and he said never. He was the one to drive the car and now has to live with this pain as part of his existence.

The decision about who would attend Steven's sentencing was awkward. Alex and Marc IV agreed to go with Marc and me. Lindsay, then thirteen, declined. Two close family friends, Tim and Diane, joined us. Another good friend said she couldn't go because she wouldn't know whom to sit with—us or the

Corsellos; she knew both families. It was an extremely difficult day for our town and one my family will never forget. As Marc and I walked into the courtroom, we saw a row of teenagers—Matt and Steven's friends—sitting behind us. It was surreal. Jules and Nan sat across from us. *Was this really happening?*

We met Mr. and Mrs. Fields, the couple in the minivan that had been side swiped by the Ferarri. My heart bled as I heard their testimony. They saw their lives pass before their eyes. They saw a car rushing toward them at lightning speed, and they thought about their two children who nearly became orphans. How could my son play such a role in this tragedy? He was in a car that almost destroyed a family. Mr. Fields was badly injured, requiring extensive physical rehabilitation. Both suffered emotional trauma and flashbacks from the crash. Both witnessed the death of my son.

My husband was too devastated to speak at the sentencing, but his profound statement was read by Onondaga County Assistant District Attorney Joanne Michaels.

> This sentence is the consequence of having no consequences, of accepting unacceptable behavior regarding teenage drinking.
>
> It has been extremely difficult for Marianne and I to accept the loss of our son, Matt, due to avoidable circumstances. There was no terminal illness, no act of God, no battle in defense of our country, and no cowardly terrorist attack to justify his death.
>
> Matt's life, which had so much promise, was just unnecessarily wasted. All the boys that evening made a decision to drink, compromising their ability to make the right decisions. Steven made the fatal decision to drink and drive. This decision has forever changed his life, his family's life, a community's life but, most importantly the lives of my family and myself.
>
> Within hours of the accident, I realized that nothing I could do would bring my son back. This is a horrific feeling

of helplessness. I also knew in my heart that Steven was suffering with us. The absence of anger and bitterness for him was replaced with sympathy.

I realized that Marianne and I could make a difference in his life if we were able to offer forgiveness and encouragement towards his healing process, which we have tried to do. While we were able to forgive, we are not responsible for justice. Forgiveness is easier to offer when there is justice, but there is no punishment that is worthy of Matt's life or the life sentence Marianne and I received the moment that Ferrari left the road.

The horrifying reality of drinking is that it is so unnecessary. However, as a society we have allowed alcohol to become a prerequisite to everything we do. We will continue to bury our loved ones unnecessarily as long as this culture continues to glorify alcohol.

—Marc Angelillo
Sentencing, June 2005

At the sentencing I found the strength and courage to say,

One year ago, I decided to leave this tragic outcome in the hands of the justice system and prayed to God He would wrap his arms around it in prayer.

Marc and I have realized that Steven's punishment would never bring Matt back nor right this wrong. We did not want Steven's punishment to be retribution for our loss, however, we both prayed the punishment would affect others in some way to alter future decisions and save other lives. We feel Steven's pain today, but also feel hope that someone is learning a lesson out there. Someone will live because of Matt Angelillo and Steven Corsello.

The Angelillo family and the Corsello family have suffered greatly this year and will continue to do so. I recognize that our burdens are enough for each of us and we cannot possibly carry each other's as well. We will

walk in our own shoes. However, please recognize that the
Corsellos can still see their son every week, we cannot."

—Marianne Angelillo
Words at Sentencing

If you could reach teenagers and try to impact them with a
horrifying consequence of drinking, this was it. Judge Aloi was
so powerful in this June 2005 courtroom scene as he addressed
the teenagers and adults in the courtroom. These words are also
used behind video clips of Matt's life in my educational video
for assemblies.

> Have we sunk so low as a society and are so tolerant of
> teenage drinking that we can cast the lives of other people
> onto a junk pile by simply offering the excuse, "This is
> what teenagers do?" I think not.
>
> Judge Aloi deals with burglars, robbers…why are we
> here, why are we in a criminal courtroom in Onondaga
> County? You may be saying that killing someone while
> driving drunk is different. It's not a serious violent crime
> at all, is it? I am here to tell you, Steven, that it is a serious
> violent crime.
>
> These are tragedies ladies and gentlemen, and we need
> to face up to them. This sentencing is about accountability,
> responsibility, and yes, appropriate punishment. But I do
> know this Steven. Matt Angelillo would gladly change
> positions with you today. Matt Angelillo was given a death
> sentence on June 19th of last year.
>
> I want to paint this picture of Matthew's death and
> others' physical injuries as a tragedy and the irreversible
> consequences of the choices you make and they make
> every day when you consciously choose to drink and then
> drive. Let Matt Angelillo's life and his death and the
> scarred lives of the other victims of your criminal conduct
> be a beacon of responsibility and accountability for your
> actions.

Judge Aloi asked the teenagers in the court to rise. He said,

> After seeing all of the pain and sorrow for everyone involved in this case, and the punishment I have just imposed upon Steven Corsello as a result of his drinking and driving…I want to ask each one of you…will you now drink and drive? Yes or no?

Could a teenager under the influence, with a still developing brain, truly anticipate the suffering they could cause by one night of partying? I don't think so! Steven rose and looked to the Angelillo family. He said,

> I would like to take this opportunity to apologize to the Angelillo family. The pain and grief I have caused are astounding. However unintentional, my friend and the Angelillos' son, is gone and won't be coming back. Every life is ultimately unique and a person can never be replaced or substituted for. That is why we praise the individual. A part of me died with Matt that night, and I know that I as well as others will never be the same. Nor should we be. Because of all this, I have gained critical insight into my reckless behavior and know that it cannot stand. The consequences are much too profound. Everyone can learn from this, especially my peers, and it is my sincere wish that they all do so.
>
> Matt filled a special place in all the lives he touched and that space will forever remain vacant. I will carry this for the rest of my life, my own grief, and my own guilt, over the manner of my friend's death. I was driving that car, and Matt is no longer with us because of me. This haunting truth will be my companion for as long as I walk this earth. Nothing I say or do can suffice for the magnitude of this tragedy. I only wish to make my feelings known about which has come to define my very existence.
>
> I feel as though merely saying sorry would be so inadequate that it could only emulate empathy. I will

apologize with my life and honor my friend with all that I do and all that he stood for. Matt was a person of many virtues, virtues that I have tried to live by in the past months. My deepest condolences will remain with the Angelillo family.

—Steven Corsello
Sentencing 2005

Judge Aloi sentenced Steven to two years in state prison. Years later, I would be contacted by a bereaved mother who faced a similar court case. She asked how we did it. She asked how to write a victim impact statement. I told her I felt a sense of healing after the sentencing. The judge validated my pain, so I sent him a note after the sentencing, thanking him for helping us heal. In the courtroom, Judge Aloi gave tribute and meaning to Matt's life and death.

Matt Angelillo is a hero to me and should be a hero to everyone in this community. Matthew's life and death—his very soul and spirit has touched the hearts and minds and the conscience of this community like no other case that I've seen. This case and his death has brought before us like no other case the senseless violent tragedy of teenage drinking and driving in this community.

—Judge Aloi
Sentencing

No one can undo how our lives have been altered. No one can stop the flow of tears, regrets, grief, or pain. No one can take away Steven's prison sentence and the impact on his life. No one can fill the void in my family, the forever empty seat at our table. But one thing can be done in Matt's memory and in recognition of the pain. It is what the judge suggested. "Let this horrific tragedy affect the conscience of communities." That has given me strength to heal and the desire to spread Matt's story in any way I can.

Seven years after the sentencing, I found myself speaking to a large audience of eighth graders. I referred to Judge Aloi's words that Matt would gladly change positions with Steven because he was given a "death sentence." I have thought an infinite number of times how much different it would be if Matt had been driving. I am not sure Matt would have gladly changed positions with Steven. I am not sure Matt could have handled the pain of causing a friend's death. I am not sure Matt would have survived such guilt. I am not sure Matt would have survived state prison. Would I have survived seeing Matt suffer so?

Matthew

Family wedding in August 2003

Marc and Matthew

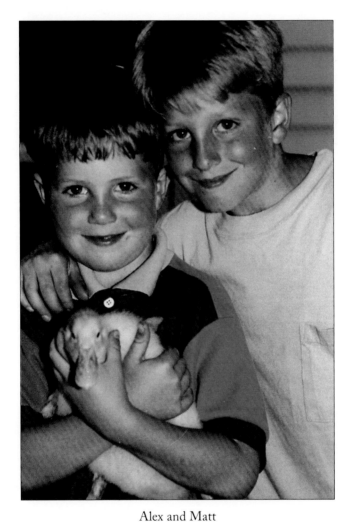

Alex and Matt

Matthew's catch of the day

Mother and son enjoy a sunset 1994

Siblings catch of the day

Florida family vacation

Matthew and Lindsay at Bloody Pond

Father and son catch

Albany football game

On the dock at Bloody Pond

Exploring the Oregon coast

Alex, Matt, and Marc on a duck hunt

Matt in lacrosse game

Matt and Alex are Latin Award winners

Forty-sixth birthday with Mom and Dad

Matt said, "Mom, get the camera!"

Lauren and Matt at junior prom

Matt and friends at junior prom

Brothers on Mother's Day 2004

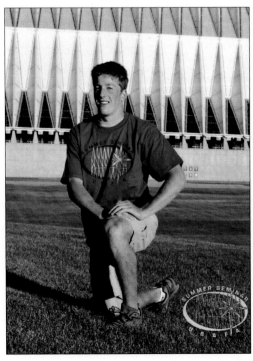

Matthew at Summer Seminar-United States Air Force Academy

What was left

Memorial at home

Healing on the "Point"

Gone4ever exhibit with Lindsay

Speaking at Fayetteville-Manlius High School

Sleep in heavenly peace

Me and Marc on Point

Alex's Naval Academy graduation

Alex and Andrea's wedding

New camp dedication

An Alien

The public nature of this tragedy divided our community. Many were appalled that a teenager could be sent to state prison for DWI. Alcohol is an extremely sensitive subject. In one of my intolerable days of pain, I called my sister, Susan, to vent. She guided me to the Bible, Ephesians 6:10 (NIV).

> So put on all of God's armor. Evil days will come.
> But you will be able to stand up to anything
> And after you have done everything you can,
> you will still be standing.

I read it through and through, and I prayed for God to help me bear the opinions.

A week after Matt's death, our family left to go back to their lives. Marc and I were officially on our own. We contemplated the boat and decided to take a ride as it was a beautiful day. We left our dock and thought, *now what?* Several of our friends had tied up their boats in the familiar cove. I said, "We should go and be with them, it will help us."

Reluctantly, Marc coasted over to join them. They were relaxing, having a good time on a beautiful day. An electric blender was roaring, and we were offered a shot of tequila. It was difficult to explain this moment of realization: our party days are over. How would we learn to fit into this old life with our new "fatal vision"?

I always considered myself a "connector" because relationships are important to me. I remember not wanting to go back to work full-time after the children were born because it would prevent us from having company on weekends. I have been a "people" person my entire life, giving friendships and family the highest priority. As Malcolm Gladwell describes a connector in his book *The Tipping Point*,[9]

> Connectors are the people in a community who know large numbers of people and who are in the habit of making introductions. A connector is essentially the social equivalent of a computer network hub. They usually know people across an array of social, cultural, professional, and economic circles, and make a habit of introducing people who work or live in different circles. They are people who "link us up with the world...people with a special gift for bringing the world together." They are "a handful of people with a truly extraordinary knack [...for] making friends and acquaintances."
>
> —*The Tipping Point* by Malcolm Gladwell

I know I have a gift to bring people together. I felt centered in most of my life with successful relationships. I prided myself on never leaving anyone out of my social networks. I never tired of entertaining. I was right where I wanted to be, in the middle of everything.

So it would make sense why this part of my grief journey was insurmountable to me. I felt isolated from so many of my good friends because I had a difficult time connecting to them. Matt's death was so complicated, and the relationship to alcohol was painful. Alcohol, which had been a simple positive thing—relating to lightheartedness, giddiness, and social affairs—now had a negative connotation. My relationship to alcohol had changed into pain and fury.

It played a major factor in our son's death. It devastated our lives. Now it complicated our healing and our social lives.

Suddenly, the words *drunk, party, alcohol,* and *underage drinking* had become painful. I couldn't bear to be around lighthearted social affairs. Hope for Bereaved recommended that you park your car by the door in social situations in case you need to escape. So we did. Both Marc and I would part from most social functions early, finding it difficult to accept a drink.

Again, I call it that "fatal vision," the different way you see things after the death of a child, especially an unnecessary death. All your priorities become rewired. Life suddenly becomes far more than just having fun. It becomes serious and emotional.

Initially, I tried to continue loving and forgiving and not to focus on how Matt died but on how he lived. But the tragedy continued to haunt me. My early journal entries were strictly about my grief and then later shifted to the enormous hole and the bad decisions that caused it.

Journal Entry 2004

Marc is dealing so courageously with lawyers, insurance agents, law enforcement, grief and stress. He's truly an amazing man and is doing all of this for our children and us. No man loves his children and family more than Marc. He's been the protector for all of us. That is one of the problems...he feels like he has failed. He was not able to protect Matthew despite the lifetime of lectures, love, praise, and criticism and curfews. Matt lost his wisdom and his core beliefs for one small evening of his life. And now he's gone forever. There's no reflection on anything which could bring him back. He failed himself. Where was our lifetime of influence and teaching? Why does life break down like this? Faith is the only answer. Faith, God's love and need for Him. You have to believe this happened for a reason. You have to have faith in the Lord and His wishes for us. Insanity is the only other resulting answer.

God Bless us as all as we deal with our loss each and every day. It's the test of a lifetime- testing soul, heart,

mind and body. Can the human spirit really recover from
something as sad and disappointing as this?

The enormity of our situation became painfully evident: How
could we ever overcome our grief? It seemed overwhelming, and
we found ourselves in a balancing act of trying to grieve, forgive,
function, and fit while taking some meaning from Matt's life
and death. As much as I wanted things to change in Skaneateles,
underage drinking continued. Kids drink. Some adults know.
And there are few—if any—consequences.

A difficult incident occurred one year after Matt's death, and
I did not handle it well. Two of Matt's close friends were caught
drinking in the summer of 2005, just before Steven's sentencing. I
was outraged. I could not stop myself from writing a very honest
letter to one of the boys, who continued to be a good friend
of Steven's. "How could you insult your good friends Steven
and Matt in this way? They are trying to instill change in our
community, and you are not helping!"

My letter caused discomfort between Matt's friends and
myself. They were insulted by it. They did not comprehend my
pain or need to save others from this pain. The notion that Matt's
death and Steven's incarceration would not change the teenagers'
desire for alcohol is daunting. Some will learn to respect alcohol
and never drink and drive, but many teens will not handle it
responsibly. It is the American way.

I was crushed at the increasing distance between some of
Matt's friends and me. Despite how hard I tried to be there for
them, some only wanted to distance themselves. I knew I had to
let go. It was only years later that I realized this distancing could
not have been avoided. I was dealing with seventeen-year-old
teens who had no idea how to lose a friend. Some would change
in memory of Matt. Some would continue reckless lifestyles to
dull their pain.

In the fall of the first year, I contacted a therapist and said to her, "I am dealing with my son's death as best as I think I can. However, I need help dealing with the disconnection from my friends and life."

It was time to weed through the complicated issues and understand human nature. But why was this so difficult? Why was my self-confidence plummeting? Why didn't I fit, why didn't people understand me, and why couldn't they hang in and support me?

I learned a lot from these sessions and went frequently for over a year. I had a choice to make. I was changing, growing, and learning a tough lesson in life. I had to accept the changes or try to fit back into my old life. This was hard, but the decision to go back would never work. Matt was gone—forever. Marc and I were changed—forever. We could not go back to our old lives and pretend that Matt's senseless death did not happen.

The abuse of alcohol had created a chasm in our life so deep and furious that unless some good purpose came of it, we would be destroyed forever. The therapist told me, "I would hate to see you try and fit where you no longer belong and risk not growing as a person."

The other meaningful message from these sessions was about "emotional IQ." We are aware of the intelligence quotient—IQ— but we rarely think about how equipped humans are to handle emotional challenges. My therapist explained that just as we are born with intelligence IQ, we are also born with emotional IQ— some high and some low.

I realized that some of the people in our lives could not handle our suffering. It is human nature for many to want to avoid suffering, and I could see this happening to many of the people in our lives. Clearly, many became uncomfortable around our grief. My therapist said, "Humans can be like animals, they leave their sick and wounded." I was encouraged to share my heart with only those who could handle it. I needed to understand and accept that others did not need to live through my grief.

I wrote a paper for Hope for Bereaved called, "Grief, Loss, and Abandonment."

> I have spent many months questioning how and why some of my relationships have not survived the test of grief and tragedy. I tried to explain to those close to me that I need two things desperately as I cope with the tragic loss of my seventeen-year-old son. I need compassion and time. I need people to tell me that they care, to call me, stop in to see me, or just spend time with me.
>
> I do not need to be judged, analyzed or advised…I need compassion and understanding. I need someone to help me pass some time as comfortably as possible.

A frustrated friend told me, "No matter what I do for you, it's never enough!" Of course it wasn't. No one could ever do enough for me. No one could fix me. I further explained,

> Yes, we are wounded and I compare the sensitivity of my heart to a painful skin disease which cannot handle anything but the softest of cotton. I have limited stamina to handle rejection, criticism, and misunderstanding. My heart is aching and I am no longer the lighthearted, easygoing soul I used to be. I walk along a windy hilly road with no warning of the twists and turns. Each day is a different day with emotional highs and lows.
>
> I should be forgiven that I am different. I should entrust myself to those who can be patient with me and love me for who I now am. I trust that someday I will wake from this nightmare called grief and realize that in a time of tragedy and loss, our sails cannot be accurately steered. The winds of grief will take us to new and different places. However, we must not be hard on ourselves but instead realize that sometimes time and prayer alone is needed to heal us.

It helped to talk with other bereaved parents. I realized from support groups, from meeting with other bereaved friends, that this disconnection is a natural circumstance.

Journal Entry
April 1st, 2005

It's been days or so since I last wrote and things have not improved. I have struggled each and everyday to drag myself through life. I'm trying to stay busy but the morning doves are out, the birds are singing and spring is coming. Lacrosse, prom, pasta dinner for the senior class—it's all happening around us as we move along. It's incredibly painful and some moments have been plain unbearable. We've gotten through so much the past nine months and we have three more to bring us to full cycle. We planned the dedication for Matt on the 22nd of May so I am shopping for a headstone and preparing the video and two speeches for DWI night. It's all awful, so painful, and my heart just aches as though it is last summer again. Will nice weather ever be enjoyable again?

We meet with our lawyer to go over Matt's death settlement and everything makes me struggle with anger and bitterness. The seniors have not been around and it seems so strange to be so alone in our grief. Once again, I guess this is what grief is all about. Loneliness.

Reading how others have dealt with grief and suffering has helped console me. One very bad day, I ended up in a bookstore at the Carousel Mall in Syracuse, standing in the self-help section, praying for the right book. One called *Grace,* by R. T. Kendall, caught my eye. I noticed the author recommended another of his book called, *Total Forgiveness.*[10] This is what I needed. I brought it home and studied it for days.

The concept of forgiveness is very complex. First, it is a choice—not a feeling. The choice most helps the one who is doing the forgiving. Also, forgiveness does not require reconciliation.

Forgiving someone does not mean you reconcile the relationship. The process of forgiving is letting go of bitterness and resentment to give you peace and healing. It is not something you have to announce. It does not require you to tell the person who has hurt you.

This person may not think they have done anything wrong. Telling them that you forgive them will just incite anger on their part. The goal is to let the negative emotions go. Then your heart is free to accept positive emotions. I wanted to forgive everyone who had hurt me. Of course, the sadness I felt toward some personal friends and family were far more difficult to forgive than the choice to forgive Steven. I had forgiven him because he never meant to hurt our son. I believed society's acceptance of alcohol was more a target to blame. Also, it is difficult to forgive those who are close to you.

Journal Entry January 2007

This was a huge step for me. I went to a luncheon with my old group of friends. I tried to be light hearted and the old "Marianne" speaking of my living children. Of course no mention of my life the past two and a half years. No mention of my son in the grave. This is the way people want it to be. This is how they want you to move forward. They just expect you to not acknowledge your life of change and suffering.

I couldn't do it for a long time but today I did it willingly and gracefully. No guilt, no bitterness, no anger, no hatred—just camaraderie and acceptance that you have to pretend nothing ever happened to you and your life. That's the way you get accepted back into your old life.

However, the good news is that I can leave, get into my car and embrace who I now am and who I like being. I will share the new me with reservation and selectivity. Wow. That's the proper end of my essay on abandonment. It took me one and a half years to be able to say it and write it and think it.

It is much easier to forgive when someone asks to be forgiven or reaches out for reconciliation. It took years, but some people have come to me and expressed regrets that they had misunderstood me. One good friend apologized, saying she mishandled my grief. She now has a much better understanding of what I went through.

Eight years later, Matt's friends began to reach out to me. I was invited recently to "friend" one of Matt's old buddies on Facebook. His note touched me. He was studying for his master's degree, doing well. I told him how happy I was for him. I sent congratulations. Six years after the death, this young man apologized for not being there for my family. He said he was embarrassed by his behavior back then, that he was immature. He said, "Matt would be proud of me today."

Looking back, I realize it was no one's fault that my life had become so complicated, so sad, so difficult. I had to do my own healing—on my own time. I had to digest how I would fit back into society and the Skaneateles community. I needed to personally deal with my anxious moments and my grief. Our good friends and family needed to go back to their own lives. My personal healing would happen in my own way.

Sharing
My Stones

I n 2005, an Alcohol and Substance Abuse committee in nearby
Cayuga County asked me to speak at its annual spring forum
on underage drinking. The members recalled my letter to the *Post-Standard* newspaper and asked me, "Will you share your pain and
save a life?" I will never forget my conflicted emotions—the fear,
courage, grief, and hope that all emerged at once.

I threw myself back into my journals, hoping to organize my
thoughts and find the right words. A journal entry dated March
23, 2005 captured them perfectly.

> Journal entry March 23, 2005
> At the Point
>
> What would I say to teenagers and to my beloved son?
> One at your age does not truly comprehend or imagine
> the full value that your life holds in this world. A teenager
> does not grasp the power his or her existence has in a
> family, in a school, in a group of friends. Yes, we are asked
> to speak because we are the ones who can truly describe
> the loss in our hearts and in our souls. How can we touch
> teenagers and make them realize how important they
> are, how truly valuable their lives are. How can we make
> everyone in this room for one minute pretend they are
> not here due to a preventable teenage accident? Can you
> allow yourselves for one minute to feel the horrible pain

it would cause your parents, siblings, friends, classmates, etc—to hear that you are gone from this world because you made a tragic decision to drive under the influence. Your bed remains empty, your locker sits idle, your school work is untouched, your jerseys hang unused, and no one knows what to do with that empty seat at the kitchen table. All your hopes and dreams are gone forever. Now visualize changing the life of everyone around you. Do you realize how much everyone depends on you? Your parents have sacrificed almost 20 years in preparing a good life for you. Your siblings have looked forward to you being by their sides for life—future weddings, children together, brothers and sisters for life—that's the way life is supposed to be. That's all gone too—your legacy will be only teenage years and hopes and dreams. Your parents have to cope with pain so horrific that it creeps into every minute of their conscious being. The void is unbearable but all must learn to live with it.

I am telling you all here that you have a huge responsibility before you each and every day you walk out that door. It is to make wise responsible decisions. It is to keep you and others safe and to appreciate every moment you are given to make a difference to those around you. This responsibility goes beyond you. It goes beyond selfish moments of careless fun and risk taking. This is a responsibility to the life you have created with the many people loving you each and every day.

What will you do in the years ahead when faced with these situations? Will you be the one to drink and drive? Will you be the one to kill a friend or innocent victim? Will you be the innocent victim to be killed by a drunken driver or will you be the friend to take the keys away from a drunken friend? I want you to be fully aware of these situations and chose the safe one.

Matthew's high school friend, neighbor, and classmate is currently serving two years in a state penitentiary for vehicular manslaughter. Matthew's death in that crash was caused by this friend, who will never be the same young man ever again. He is faced with three felony counts and a prison term forcing him to reflect on his pain, his loss and his guilt over poor choices.

I also poured over video clips of Matthew because I wanted to show a music video of Matt's life. I selected samples of clips to show his personality, his love of the outdoors, his friends, and his siblings. I wanted everyone to get to know Matt well and to show what we had lost. I wanted my audience to understand the hole in our lives.

I told my family, "I think I have blown some kind of emotional fuse." My strength even amazed myself. I believed in a divine intervention so I gave credit to the *Holy Spirit* for the inner strength to share Matt's story. I also felt support from my family for my mission of sharing Matt's story with high school audiences.

In the spring of 2006, I was asked to address an auditorium full of students from several high schools around Syracuse. I carefully prepared my words. I spent hours working on a video about Matt's life and death, alternating clips from home video and the TV news coverage. I still don't know how I was able to relive the tragedy over and over again, but I knew that I had to do it.

Alex agreed to be my narrator. The idea stemmed from his essay for the National Honor Society.

> I miss my brother. He was my best friend. We shared a bedroom for fifteen years. There are so many memories of him in here. I watched him work hard to improve himself and he gave me the motivation to do the same. His dreams however have disappeared. I have used his death to guide me in my life, to help me make the right choices and to help others make the right choices. This is his story.
>
> —Alex Angelillo

I believe in the power of stories. I believe in the power of sharing.

So many stories have been handed down forever, with many lessons initially coming from the Bible. Jesus Christ spoke parables to educate and illustrate a point. Many people tell their stories in newspapers, books, and movies. We all have so much to learn from each other.

Matt's story is captivating. I like to think that it perhaps is due to Matt's great smile, his blue eyes, his personality, or maybe his family. A student once came up to me after an assembly and said, "I miss him already."

I realize the healing nature of sharing. Hope for Bereaved provides such necessities when it comes to grief. Hope for Bereaved encourages sharing those sorrowful stones, and as I handed my stones to all those students over the years, I definitely felt a lot of grief lift from me.

I tell myself that Matthew's purpose is different from what I expected. He will not go to college, he will not be attending the Air Force Academy, he will not marry or have children, and he is not able to sit at my dinner table. But I like to believe that God's purpose for his life is still profound and essential to this world. He is saving lives even though I may never know which ones.

Consistently across the board, the students who seek me out afterward are the ones who have experienced suffering. They just get it. They have immense compassion for me and want to share their own suffering. My heart aches for those so young who had to experience loss or pain. I had lived many happy years before knowing about true suffering. How sad for teens so young to know so much about it.

I met one young man who had spent two weeks in a coma after an accidental drug overdose. He came so close to death but now has totally changed his life for the better. We have crossed speaking paths, shared lunch, and worked together on a video for the community called *Parents, You Can't Afford to be Clueless!* He totally understands! His suffering is being used for the betterment of society as he is sharing his stones. He is healing and will be stronger for it all.

Another student comes to mind who found me after an assembly and said to me, "Mrs. Angelillo, I only wish my mother was here. She has had a few DWIs and I tell her to remember Matt. I wish she would just get it." This is such amazing insight for a young teenager. Another student came up to me to tell me that his father was "not a bad drunk driver" because he had not experienced a consequence yet. Does that make him a good drunk driver? Wow…

As I have continued to speak in the northeast, my opportunities to reach teens have been amazing. I recently spoke at one school where they had just lost a senior to a suicide. I encouraged everyone in the audience to be aware of the power of sharing their sorrow, to speak about it, and they will feel their load lighten. I was amazed at the exchanges I had with several students after the assembly. One young man told me he had lost his dad when he was ten and it felt good to talk about this loss with me. Another young man wanted to share the pain of losing his grandmother. I asked them, "You feel like an alien at times, don't you?" and they both said YES!

One student recently met with me after an assembly to "share her stones." She had lost a sibling in a four-wheeler crash and had also lost an aunt and a beloved friend. She wanted to know why such bad things happened to her. She wanted to know why everyone was dying around her. Once again, I had to be strong and reassure her that bad things do happen to good people. No one is exempt from suffering. My biggest advice is to fill that horrible hole with only one thing and one thing only, *love*! It is so important to keep on loving because love is such a powerful healing emotion.

School assemblies are a gift to me because I have a captive audience of teens with whom I can share pertinent messages. I often bring in a few of Matt's belongings and point to them on a table and say, "These are just 'things' you leave behind, which really don't mean anything. The most important things you leave behind are the relationships you have made and how well you have touched hearts and lives while you were here. Matt is 'gone4ever.' The problem is we don't know how long forever is. What is your forever? Is it forty years, ten years, or a day? Don't let your forever be cut short by an instance of teenage recklessness."

I have communicated with many teens over the years both in person and e-mail. This is one small sample of the many notes I have received over the years. It speaks volumes to me that Matt has that right smile, blue eyes, and impish grin to impact students.

> Hey, I'm a senior at Chittenango. I talked to you a little bit after you told my school your story and I just wanted to thank you for your beautiful presentation you gave today. I wish I could be as strong as you are about your son. I know everyone is different with dealing with death, and everyone grieves differently. It feels like time has gone by so slow, but fast at the same time since my friend lost his life. I can't even imagine what you're feeling and have been dealing with for six years, but you are truly doing a great job. Being strong is so hard to do at times like that, but you are one of the strongest people I know. I hope you keep on talking to teenagers, and families. It helped me so much. Keep staying strong, and thank you again so much.
>
> Sincerely,
Student
Chittenango High School

My other favorite part of speaking is getting to meet our amazing administrators and teachers. Central New York is blessed with such caring, interesting, and strong educators. It takes a lot of courage to orchestrate these presentations. Many schools take their pre-prom assemblies extremely seriously. One school even stages a tragedy in order to impact their student body. Called, "Every 15 Seconds," this mock DWI brings the realistic pain and horror of a DWI crash. I was asked to end the program two different years. For me, this was one of the most emotional assemblies because in their video, I had to sit and witness the parents and students walking in my shoes for a brief day. It was heart wrenching to watch, but I applauded them for trying to make the recreation real.

One principal sat with me after my presentation and discussed the sensitive nature of underage drinking with parents. He said, "You have to make them uncomfortable." I guess this is the difficulty we are facing in order to change society and attitudes. We have to make people feel uncomfortable.

> Marianne Angelillo presented her son Matthew's story at Oneida High School this past year. Her grace and centered presences emanated through our audience of eight hundred students and faculty. Marianne has a true gift. As a mother telling her story of their family's tragedy, she was able to touch the hearts and minds of our students.
>
> Our audience's emotion and standing ovation for Marianne speaks volumes of her courage to relive their family's story with the outcome of helping others
>
> On behalf of the Oneida family, Marianne, we thank you for sharing your stones.
>
> —Brian Gallagher, Principal
> Oneida High School.

My assemblies are never the same even though my reason for sharing is always the same. The way an assembly goes depends on the day, the mood, and the emotions of everyone. Sometimes I am strong, sometimes I am weak, and sometimes I lack confidence. However, the reason I stand up and share is because I believe this story has the power to impact students and change their attitudes. This summarizes it in one of my talks.

> The pain these tragedies cause is astounding. We all suffer; Matt's family, the driver's family and the entire community of Skaneateles. I have spent the last few years reflecting on this new thing in my life called grief. As I have seen firsthand, we all grieve in our own way. There is really no right or wrong way to grieve. However, I am sure about

one thing. If I am to make any sense out of the loss of my son, I must face the pain and the true reason why he is no longer with us. The pain will not kill us, but running from it might. Matt is no longer with us because of underage drinking, teenage risk taking and poor choices.

I wrote in my journal after the tragedy the following, "Letters are coming in for Matthew and they are tucked away in his memory book. They represent an individual who had purpose, drive, energy and a true crave to share whatever he envisioned with all who came in contact with him." Matt did motivate many and could have been an inspiration if he carried on. But then I think in a lot of ways he can and still be an inspiration. His friends are testaments to that because they will never forget him; but what about all the young teenagers and children who never got a chance to be touched by his energy and drive? Can they still be given an opportunity to learn from Matthew and his tragic situation? That is why I am here today. I believe Matt can continue to touch lives through his tragedy. The greatest tragedy is not death, but life and death without purpose. The only thing more tragic than losing Matt, is no lessons learned by others.

—Assembly Talk to High School 2006

I have encouraged my family to believe in the power of sharing stones. One year on Matt's birthday I called Alex at school to ask how he was doing. I wanted to know if he found anyone to talk to about Matt that day. He said to me, "Mom, no one wants to hear about that!" I responded with "Alex, that's where you are wrong. There are people out there who would love to talk to you about Matt. You just have to recognize them." I tell students it may not be your best friend, it may not be someone you are close to, but there is someone out there who will find it a privilege to take one of your stones.

A Family's Hole

1/17/05

I miss Matt terribly and especially his life. His friends continue to be accepted to college and his college mail continues to arrive. We recently received another letter from Congressman (James) Walsh recognizing their loss and our tragedy. The Air Force Selection committee dedicated their nomination process to Matthew. We are so proud of what could have been for our son.

Graduation for the class of 2005 at Skaneateles High School was a surreal event for us. Marc and I agreed: We needed to get out of town. We could not watch Matt's class graduate without him. We planned a weekend trip to a beautiful outdoor preserve owned by friends. We invited family and friends to come.

I spent that Saturday morning hand-delivering graduation cards and a video of "Matt moments" I had collected. I couldn't think of any other gift. It was appropriate to share my son and give them memories of their good friend.

We all were experiencing the difficulty of moving forward without Matt. One single week brought the one-year anniversary of the crash (along with Father's Day), Steven's sentencing in court, and the high school graduation. I don't know how we survived it. We continued to love each other, to love our families, and to live in the present as best we could. The nature preserve was incredible, and I wrote in my journal about our positive energy and thoughts of gratitude.

June 25th 2005 at Savannah Dhu

It has been an incredible experience getting to bring the family here. It has been the most perfect diversion for all of us. Graduation day in Skaneateles bothered me all year and now is a distant thought—we are surrounded by family and friends once again. The Congels have graciously donated use of this world-class nature compound and we have appreciated every minute of their love and generosity. *Wow* is all I can say. I have enjoyed seeing a happy and excited face on Marc and would give anything to have this side of his personality stay forever—but how can we divert our life every day and every minute?

I was so happy to be sharing a serene environment with close friends and family. I was back to my camera, capturing the love of the weekend and the incredible environment. Nature is so healing to one's soul, and this preserve was the perfect place to divert our pain. It worked. We were forever thankful to survive one of the most challenging weekends a human being could have to process.

There was relief in sight when the sentencing was done and Matt's class was now headed for college. The new school year began throwing us into life once again. I could move forward, diverted with the activities of my other children. In the fall, I videotaped Alex's football season and actually was able to enjoy it. I could still picture number 29 on the field, but now Alex was giving me so much joy. I went through another season of team dinners, videotaping games, and cheering on the Lakers. Alex helped me on the year-end highlight film. It seemed life was a bit lighter, and I attributed the changes to a new memory bank.

I wrote a paper to Hope for Bereaved called, "Creating New Memories." It describes why the first year of loss is so incredibly painful. One must go through 365 days of "firsts" without your loved one. The first Christmas, Thanksgiving, birthday, vacation, mall trip, and what one fellow bereaved mother coined "angelversary" (anniversary of death). It is a long, painful year during which you just hold your breath as you cross the days off the calendar. There is no relief. It just needs to be over.

Journal entry:

One year ago my memory bank caused intense suffering. Every thought I had revolved around my life that included my beloved son, Matthew. I saw his Honda sitting in the driveway, his empty bed in his room, his football and lacrosse equipment in the garage, and then a host of his friends gathered down the street at the neighbors. My daily thoughts that were processing my life all included Matthew.

He was my son for seventeen years and he had lived in my home by my side. I fed him, clothed him, taught him, and loved him. I watched his every move in my life. He was an integral part of my memory bank and everything I had experienced since he was born. His place at my table, his face in my family photos and videos, his laugh and smile, were all part of my last seventeen years on this earth. So, no wonder the pain is so intense and so difficult to steer from. Every memory I had on the morning of June 20th, 2004 included him.

That autumn, I tried to explain an uplifting feeling I experienced.

I realized on my bike this beautiful morning why I am feeling better after one devastating year. My mind can now process new memories, which no longer include Matthew. It's ok for my mind to wander to the events of this year, some of which were new happy times to celebrate. I spent wonderful long weekends with family and friends. There was a trip to Saratoga to the racetracks, a wonderful family gathering at Savannah Dhu, beautiful days on the lake, and many photos and videos all created in the last fourteen months.

I have new music to listen to, new recipes to cook, and even a new neighbor to chat with. Yes, my memory bank has gotten bigger and includes new memories of events, people, and places, which do not all include my beautiful son, Matthew. Many of them include people I love and cherish. Yes, I miss Matt terribly and ache for our loss, but one year ago I was not sure life was worth living without my son. The pain was so severe I counted the minutes until each day would pass. Therese Schoeneck from "Hope for Bereaved" of Syracuse promised me in that first very painful but productive meeting that the grief would soften.

I can now look back on the last fourteen months and offer others hope that the pain does soften over time. The memory bank gets new life and new thoughts; you change and your heart becomes enlarged for all those who suffer. I will always love my son and will always have his presence in my heart and mind, but I know it's all right to carry on.

In Jerry Sittser's, *A Grace Disguised*, he calls the new memories that are created "gifts of grace."

These gifts of grace will come but we have to realize that it will require a kind of sacrifice, the sacrifice of believing that however painful our losses, life can still be good, good in a different way than before but good nevertheless.

—Jerry Sittser
A Grace Disguised

Each year without a loved one forces you to create new memories, without them. However, the difficult part, which worsens every year, is how much you miss them. At times, it gets to be too much to bear. What would Matt look like today? What would he be doing? Would he be at the Air force Academy playing lacrosse?

Kenny Chesney released a beautiful song called "Who You'd Be Today." I remember being on my way to visit a good friend of Matt's after this friend had surgery. When I heard the words to the song, I had to pull the car over to the side of the road. The words probably resonate with every bereaved person in the world as this song describes all the feelings and thoughts of losing a loved one prematurely.

February 21, 2005
At Tim and Michelle's

We have cried a lot on this vacation and have had too much time to think. Our tragedy and loss of Matthew is breaking our hearts with such force—like it happened yesterday. I asked Alex if he missed Matt in Florida and he responded, "I miss Matt everywhere."

I think of Matt in everything I do and see here. The hot tub he loved to go in with me, the cameras he loved to share my passion over, the fish he caught and cooked, and the food he so devoured. I ache, missing him every minute. It breaks my heart to watch Alex's loneliness. It's not easy to witness as he lost his partner in life. I realize how they did everything together—catching lizards, watching movies, fishing, eating, and swimming. It hurts to witness this solitary son on vacation.

Someone asked me recently what my breaking point of this loss is. It wasn't hard to answer. I responded quickly, "Alex's pain. I can't handle it." My heart broke for Matt's brother, Alex. Certainly, all my children were devastated by this loss, but as Alex would say in one of his essays, "I was closest to Matt in my family."

August 30, 2007

For the first week following Matt's death, we had the support of all our relatives and friends who helped to ease the pain. We reminisced about memories of holidays together and camping trips on Lake George. We remembered Matt in everything, and we knew him only as the blue eyed, energetic, young boy who was always giving my mother a "nervous breakdown." But eventually, the wheels began to turn on our lives, the relatives and loved ones left, and we were alone with each other and our unspeakable grief. Once I went back to work at the vineyard that summer, it was as if life had just moved on despite our protest. Days at work and nights at football practice, by the time I retired at night I had not the energy to make any sort of social effort. I remembered Matt most when I was alone. In the early mornings driving the farm's golf cart down to the main house, the five-minute trip seemed an eternity. I thought of how much I missed Matt. All of the promises of his life: the straight A's, the varsity letters, his excitement from just getting back from summer seminar at the Air Force Academy, all vanished that night. The cool morning air made the tears, which often came forth seem colder. It always ended though, and work always followed. I prayed at night to see him again, to go back to that day and change his fate; nevertheless, life pulled on me, straining to hold on to those days I wanted back.

—Alex Angelillo
"Amor Fratrium"

The absence of Matt from Alex's life was excruciating. I did not know how to mask the hole. Alex did not want the twin bed removed from his room. I decided to leave Matt's schoolbooks and notes in a bin beside his bed. My friends made a quilt out of Matt's worn T-shirts, which lies on Matt's bed. I tried to get Alex to talk about his pain, but he rarely let anyone in. The most I learned about how he was doing was in the very eloquent and passionate essays he wrote at school. The first one was called "Catullus," which Alex's high school Latin teacher, Mr. Finnegan, sent to me. The essay assignment was to find someone in history with whom you could relate the most. My heart ached as I read the words on the paper. Catullus, the poet, lost his brother in 59 BC.

June 1, 2006

In Catullus' poem 68, the poet responds to a request by his friend, Manlius, for new poetry. Catullus offers a glum explanation for why he has not produced any new poetry lately. Around 59 BC, as is estimated, Catullus' brother died suddenly. The shock of the death stunned Catullus, and he writes that he felt unable to write poetry for a while. In the poem, specifically lines 15–32, perhaps my favorite passage of all Catullus' poetry, he explains how his life was turned upside-down by the tragedy. I feel that this section of poem 68, when Catullus explains how he was overwhelmed with grief over his brother's death, touched me very strongly.

On June 20, 2004, my older brother, Matt, was killed in a car accident; he was the passenger of a drunk driver. My family was floored by the tragedy. I personally felt that all of the joys that I expected to experience throughout my life were suddenly gone. Catullus writes, "Since the time which the first pure toga was handed down to me, when my pleasant age was keeping its flowery springtime, I played the lover often enough" (tempore...lusi). Just as Catullus felt that he was in the prime of his life, playing "the lover" often enough, I felt that I was playing the "teenager" often enough. I was looking forward to summers with my friends, and a carefree high school career, when suddenly I felt that it had all disappeared. Catullus explains this exactly, when he writes, "But this brotherly death stole from me all this zeal because of my grief." Just as Catullus' passion for writing was gone, so was my passion for having a good time.

In lines 19–26, Catullus mourns the death of his brother. He writes, "Oh brother, stolen from poor me..." (O...mihi). I feel a strong connection between me and the poet, as we both did not experience a long, suffering end to a life, but a sudden and completely unexpected one. The word "stolen" echoes in my heart; it wasn't fair that we had to experience this grief. Catullus writes that his whole home was buried with his brother, that all of his family's joys died with him, and that his brother's death shattered his blessings (21–23).

I myself was the closest to my brother in my family; we had shared a room for all of the 15 years that I had been alive. We had fun together, spending our time fishing and hunting with my dad and eldest brother, Marc. I still enjoy those same things, but I think that a part of me died with Matt, although I do see the outdoors as a way to feel that he is with me. I know that everyone in my family has experienced the grief in a different way, but we all feel that some part of us is missing; there's a void where there once was Matt.

The next few lines show another side of the grieving process: some feelings of anger, irritability. Catullus says that Manlius, and perhaps other friends who were unaware of the situation, had said that Catullus should be out living his life, while he was with his family, grieving the loss of his brother. Catullus says that this action "is not shameful, it is more pitiful" (id, Mani…miserum est). Catullus apologizes sarcastically, saying that "you will excuse me if I do not bestow to you these gifts, which grief takes away from me, since I am unable [to write poetry]" (Ignosces…nequeo). This theme also "hits home" with me. Unfortunately, whether it is right or wrong, drinking is an inevitable reality of being a teenager. Since Matt's death, I have vowed not to partake in activities which will threaten my life in such a way. My friends, even my closest friends, although they were initially supportive of my decision, did continue to question my actions, wondering why I do not get back into the life that I had originally planned on living. I have little patience for these people. I, just as Catullus, feel somewhat annoyed; we both felt that the reasons behind our actions were obvious.

It is strange, if not somewhat eerie, to think that someone over two thousand years ago was experiencing the same thing that I am right now, and in the exact same ways. Catullus, at the young age of about 25, experienced the sudden loss of his brother, just as I did at fifteen. We both were emotionally paralyzed by the deaths, not expecting to experience any more pleasure for the rest of our lives. We both experienced unbearable grief, and became irritated when we were expected to just pick up the pieces of our life and be happy again.

It is this strong connection between Catullus and me that makes this passage my favorite of the year. Although it is common to feel that life is over after the death of a loved one, I would have advised Catullus against this perception; pain subsides, and although you will forever miss and love the one you lost, you will reflect on the good times you had with them, and you will feel that they are right there with you.

—Alex Angelillo
Dolor Fratris

I kept a watchful eye on Alex throughout his remaining two years of high school. I showered love on him whenever I could, realizing that I had twice the love to give. I watched him grow into Matt's body. Some days, from the back, you could not tell which son it was.

While working on the video for Alex's high school graduation, an unexpected source of gratitude came my way. I realized that beautiful clips of life were continuing despite the loss of Alex's brother. Alex never gave up. Not only did he not give up, he thrived—for his brother, for himself, and for all of us. He graduated close to first in his class, adored a special girl friend through high school, and continued to walk into many of Matt's classes and memories.

My heart ached for him as he went up to that bedroom each night to study without his brother. He never complained or showed emotion, unless you asked to talk about it. He rarely could go there. But I was thrilled when I found his writing, which confirmed to me that he was doing all right. Life was painful, but he made a choice to go on. It was a difficult and confusing time, but he sought nomination to the United States Naval Academy, and he received an appointment in the spring of 2007. His graduation from Skaneateles High School coincided with the third anniversary of Matt's death. In the closing of the ceremony, Alex addressed his class.

> I'd like to first of all thank everybody for gathering today to celebrate the success of the 2007 graduating class. It's amazing to see our community coming together today on this: the brightest day of our high school careers. What's even more amazing, however, is how our community, and especially these classmates of mine, can come together to support each other on some of our darkest days. Just over three years ago, I lost my brother Matt in a car accident, and I wasn't sure if I would be able to overcome this tragedy. But it was in those hardest days that I realized I not only had my family for comfort, but an entire community. The support I received from my friends was what carried me when I most needed to be. Life has adversity in store for everyone, and though some may not have experienced it yet, we all will in time.
>
> Never forget this class, and never believe that our friendships, though they may wane and life may lead us in different directions; never believe that they have ended; for the friends whom you will remember celebrating all the good times with, are the same friends who will show up on your doorstep to share your burdens when you need someone the most. For the twelve years that I've lived in Skaneateles, it's been an honor to know and to create unforgettable memories with each and every one of you. Thank you all.
>
> —Alex Angelillo
> Closing Remarks to the class of 2007

That June, shortly after his graduation, we delivered Alex to the United States Naval Academy. I will never forget walking away from my son—with his young, lean stature, shaved head, and those big, ugly, black glasses that framed his face. His look was forlorn and terrified. It mirrored ours. This was such a huge step, separating from another son. I had to remind myself that we were not saying good-bye to Alex forever, just for a summer of plebe boot camp. As we drove away from Annapolis, Maryland, I pulled out my journal.

Journal Entry June 29th, 2007

Alex went from a big fish in a little sea to a little fish in a sea of plebes. He shrunk before my very eyes, but I realize the Naval Academy will make him a man—a big fish once again. The process has just begun and it is going to be a long, hard one. I believe the pride we feel for him will pull all of us through this. We have not lost him like Matt; we can think of him doing real things with real people in real places. He is not in an unimaginable place like heaven or in dreams.

I felt very afraid I wouldn't be able to spot him in a sea of white uniforms. It was too familiar, the ache of wanting to hold him and hug him like I do Matt everywhere I go. I ache to see Matt in a dream, in a prayer, or in a sacred place like church or on a mountain.

I will see Alex for real, for sure, and it will not be in a dream. I did not get to hug him again and rub his hands and feel his face and head. He's here though, he's real, and he's not in heaven. He's just in the Navy.

In the fall of 2004, after that tumultuous summer, Marc IV had to try and resume his life at the University of Albany. Fortunately, he was supported by many of his football teammates.

I will never forget the Albany football team showing up at Matt's funeral and then to a lunch at our home afterwards. I told my kitchen helpers to bring out all the food we had and to feed these wonderful young men. I was amazed at the emotional support Marc IV received from his fine teammates.

He was interviewed for an article later in our *Auburn Citizen* headlined, "Knowing What a Real Loss Feels Like."[11]

> Only 21, the two-times letter winner has experienced something that helps him keep a bad grade on a exam, a looming project deadline or a loss on the football field in perspective. That's because he knows the difference between losing a football game and losing a brother.
>
> "It was very painful, it was hard to let it all sink in right there and then. It probably didn't hit me for a couple of weeks. From the time it all happened, it was hard to even think about what was going on in my life. It completely takes up everything that you think about. But not a day goes by that I don't think about my brother. I have a lot of great memories. I think about all the positive times I spent with my brother. My Mom's always been into taking pictures and videos so I have a lot of great memories with that."
>
> Marc describes his team like a family and says, "I think it helped me a lot being around the guys on the football team and having a lot of close friends on the football team. It helped me get through the day. Anyone on the football team you could go to with a problem and they would be willing to help you out."
>
> —*Auburn Citizen*
> 10/11/2005

Marc IV had the support of an amazing coaching staff. Between the team and a sensitive, loving college sweetheart, his heart was well cared for. I had asked once, "Marc, how is your heart doing?" He responded, "Mom, as long as yours is okay, mine is okay."

We went to visit him frequently in college. I was taken aback when I saw the memorial to his brother in his room. The photos, collages, and images of Matt were everywhere. He embraced my way of grieving, choosing to be surrounded by the memories. He would be okay. I found him a willing partner to discuss grief, sadness, and his brother at any time. Marc IV and I were always able to share deep feelings about our loss. He would become one of those who could keep Matt alive in his heart.

Marc IV's work ethic remained a priority, even after the death. He never missed a workout. Long-time Albany coach Bob Ford said, "He was down, that was understandable. But if anything, he seemed to have a greater resolve and determination."

Marc IV would find gyms all over the country to keep up with his athletic prowess. He played four years of football at Albany. At a road game against the University of Monmouth in New Jersey, our entire extended family showed up to support him. My brother organized a tailgate party, bringing his pickup truck with a huge banner called "The Marc Angelillo Fan Club." That day, I videotaped the game, along with many memories of this large, loving, supportive family. We were moving through life together, knowing that love would keep us going.

Lindsay's grief was a bit different from that of her brothers. Being only thirteen, she would live at home for six more years, two of them as an only child. More than anyone else, she witnessed her parents' suffering. This complicated her healing process. Lindsay and I were always close, so it was almost impossible to hide my pain from her. Unfortunately she suffered right along with us.

Lindsay was much like me and needed to process her grief. I found a handwritten letter describing the night Matt died.

> It was Saturday morning and I was excited to see Matt because he was home from the camp he was at for a week. I went downstairs and Matt was looking through his bag from the Air Force Academy, while he was talking to his friend, Greg LaForte, about his week. I gave Matt an

excited greeting but I did not hug him. (I wish I did now though). He said, "Hi Bindser!"

I asked him how it was and he said, "awesome!" I listened to him tell Greg how his week was at the Academy and then I heard him say something about going to our camp that night. Matt went upstairs to get dressed and I went online. Thirty minutes later the phone rang. It was for Matt as usual, so I ran outside to get him. I was wearing mesh shorts, a t-shirt and no shoes because I remember stepping on a rock and hurting my foot. I yelled, "Matt, phone!" He was about to get into a car and was halfway down the driveway. That was the last time I ever saw Matt.

—Lindsay Angelillo
Journal

Like me, Lindsay lost the gift to sleep. For years, she never made it through the night. I would find her on the floor of our bedroom in the morning. Something terribly wrong hit her in the middle of the night as it tortured both of us for years. I read to her messages of hope and at the time was reading Rick Warren's *Purpose Driven Life*. It was advanced for a thirteen-year-old, but the words comforted both of us as we struggled to get through those first few months.

Lindsay's eighth-grade class had learned about grief far too soon. Shortly after Matt's death, a classmate committed suicide. This brought yet another sorrowful funeral to the community. I attended the wake with Alex and Lindsay, trying to block out the still-raw memories of Matt's funeral. Months later, there was yet another funeral for a parent of one of Lindsay's friends. It was a tough time for our entire community but especially for this eighth-grade class.

One spot of hope was the middle school guidance counselor, Mr. Viggiano, or Mr. Vig to everyone. Compassionate and loving to students, he hosted group discussions, luncheons, and snacks while maintaining an open-door policy for students. I attribute much of Lindsay's healing and her ability to move forward in school and in sports to this young father who encouraged communication and "sharing stones." When Lindsay graduated from middle school, she gave Mr. Vig a signed baseball by Yogi Berra. She loved Mr. Vig and made sure he knew how much she appreciated his guidance and compassion.

Of my children, Lindsay was the most like Matt in personality. She carried a torch for him in many ways, including playing hockey and lacrosse. She loved athletics and especially the camaraderie of sports. We spent her high school years travelling with the girls' hockey team all over New York State. They were great years, and I once again collected video clips of priceless memories.

You would find evidence of Lindsay's love for her brother in the strangest ways and places. One long night, when I slept with her, I looked up to see a photo of her and Matt taped to the underside of her headboard. She was sad to find so few photos of her with Matt, but those she found were planted in her room and in her heart.

Years later, in the spring of 2009, I would be collecting clips of this brother and sister together for a video for Lindsay's high school graduation. They revealed the love Matt had for Lindsay her whole life. She spoke of a poignant Dave Matthews Band song called "Sister," which I used in the clips. The lyrics read,

> Passing time with you in mind
> It's another quiet night
> I feel the ground against my back
> Counting stars against the black
>
> I think about another day
> Wishing I was far away
> Wherever I dreamed I was
> You were there with me

Sister, I hear you laugh
My heart fills full up
Keep me please
Sister, when you cry
I feel your tears running down my face
Sister, Sister keep me

I hope you always know it's true
I would never make it through
You could make the sun go dark
Just by walking away
Playing like we used to play
like it would never go away
I feel you beating in my chest
I'd be dead without

Sister, I hear you laugh
My heart fills full up
Keep me please
Sister, when you cry
I feel your tears running down my face
Sister, Sister keep me

I hope you always know it's true
I would never make it through
You could make the heavens fall
Just by walking away

I don't think there was a dry eye in the house when the images of Matt and Lindsay appeared on the TV screen. About one hundred friends and family had gathered in our family room to watch a brother and sister share a life gone by. Dave Matthews Band was softly speaking about the love and sorrow between a brother and sister. Thank you, Dave Matthews, for speaking about such painful emotions and allowing a family to cry. I do believe Matt feels Lindsay's tears running down his face.

Dave Matthews has been an interesting influence on my family. His album *Crash* was released in April 1996, coinciding with our first year in Skaneateles. Matt introduced us to the album. We played it constantly and began following the band. We burned a CD for our annual trips to Florida to visit Grandma and Grandpa. Matt was in charge, using his birthday money to buy the town's first-ever CD burner. I remember going to the mall with Matt and being amazed that such a thing existed, wondering if Matt really knew how to run it. With the help of his dad, he installed it in that scary inside of our computer and soon was burning CD mixes for all of us. *Crash* will always remind me of Matt and this time of our life.

Matt would study up in his bedroom with Dave Matthews blasting at decibels unknown to man. Marc and I could not fathom how Dave Matthews made it easier to learn Latin and microbiology. When looking for a good song to go with a video, I would consult with Matt. Typically, he could come up with a good choice to tell the perfect story. I always used a Dave Matthews song for my children's graduation videos. I searched high and low for the perfect music to accompany Marc IV's nature video. I could not find a song that was not about love, girls, or drinking but sure enough, Matt introduced me to Dave Matthews' "Lie in Your Grave." There could not have been a more perfect match as Dave Matthews describes walking by water.

There were other children's videos with Dave Matthews' "#41" for Alex's nature scenes. Matt and I spoke about using Matthews' "Everyday" for his high school graduation video or the lacrosse team's final song because we both loved it. But it ended up to be the song choice for his funeral video.

In the spring of 2004, Matt purchased his first concert ticket, to see Dave Matthews Band in Rochester that summer. On the night of June 19, many of Matt's friends were attending the Saratoga Performing Arts Center concert in Saratoga Springs. Their cell phones delivered news of the tragedy. Matt's ticket to the Dave Matthews' concert in Rochester was given to his girlfriend, Lauren.

In the summer of 2005, my son Marc and his girlfriend took Alex and Lindsay to their first Dave Matthews concert at SPAC. I was excited for them to celebrate Matt's special band—in Matt's memory. The next year, I accompanied Lindsay to see this band for myself. I loved every minute of the "Matt moments" this band was able to bring me. Lindsay and I shared real tears when Matthews sang "Everyday." There were other Skaneateles friends, including Lauren, to share the moment with. That song still brings heartache to many of us in Skaneateles.

It was not a coincidence to me when Alex brought home his first car, and I looked at the license plate. He said, "No, Mom, I did not buy this license plate, it came with the car." The initials across the plate read, "DMB" (Dave Matthews Band). Thanks, Matt, for this gift! There were Matt gifts everywhere and everyday, but this license plate was an incredible fate. I figured that the chances of getting DMB are three out of twenty-six to the third, which is 3 out of $26 \times 26 \times 26$!

Bereaved Parents

Journal Entry 10/8/04

My friend and I went to the grave only to see a man in a baseball cap intensely visiting my son. It was Matt's father. I am feeling ready to take on some of Marc's pain. If I could, I would. Seeing him suffer has added to my burden astronomically.

I now know why it is said that losing a child is the worst thing to happen to anyone. First of all, our children are always expected to outlive us. You never imagine having to live without them or to miss out on all the life experiences they will bring into your life. I now know why it is the hardest thing for a couple to live through. You not only suffer immeasurably from missing your child, but you watch the person you have loved most, your spouse and co-parent, grieve and suffer, and there is nothing you can do about it.

The week after Matt died, good friends warned us, "Marriages often don't make it after the death of a child." At the time, I was irate that anyone would even suggest such a thing. Marc and I had a good marriage and, at the time, were extremely close and solid. We had a thirty-year relationship. How sad to think that anything could tear us apart.

July 30th 2004 at Lake George Camping

Marc and I agreed on something this morning. When the pain is the greatest, you really don't care about living or dying. There are terrible dark moments when you cannot fathom living with this pain, living without Matthew forever. However, after struggling for days with this burden, something breaks and you have calm moments, inner numbness, and you go on.

Marc and I have supported each other and all of our problems and pain for thirty years. This is the first time we have nothing good to say. We cannot help each other.

Marc and I have been together since freshman year at the University of Delaware. Remembering my first dance with Marc and that unbelievable secure feeling I had in his arms in 1975 still makes me feel passionate. Marc always took care of me. I remember coming out of class once in a downpour. I found him waiting for me in his station wagon, the "Silver Bullet."

We matured together and made sure our goals coincided. I turned down an exciting career opportunity with Kodak in Rochester so I could return to New Jersey and be close to Marc. I knew we were good for each other and would eventually get married.

I recognized a wonderful partner, friend, soul mate and future father, and I did not want to risk losing him in a long-distance romance. I found work with Bell Telephone in a difficult area in East Orange, New Jersey, where I had to face dangerous highways on snowy days and neighborhoods where losing a car stereo or more was commonplace.

But Bell Telephone was rewarding and good not only financially, but also for my confidence as I branched out and met new people. It provided a financial foundation for Marc and me in our early years.

Marc and I married in 1981 while living in New Jersey. We got an apartment in Lake Hiawatha and shared our lives with our big families living close by. However, when Marc was offered a position to work for A. Duie Pyle in West Chester, Pennsylvania, we thought the move would be good for us. I transferred to Bell of Pennsylvania in Philadelphia. We loved the Chester County area because it was horse and farm country. We were passionate about the outdoors and wanted the same dream in life, our children, a yellow lab, and a fireplace to keep warm. We worked hard and bought our first house in Exton, Pennsylvania. I needed a train station to commute to the center city of Philadelphia, so we picked the least congested area we could find. For a few years and through months of pregnancies, I made the long commute, the sixty-hour week. After Marc IV was born, I returned to work. But after Matt came, I could not go back to that lifestyle, and it was a decision I will never regret.

Even though the pros and cons sheet supported my job and earning potential, my heart was not in a job or a career. After months of my agonizing, a boss who was also a good friend helped me make my decision. She said, "Whatever you decide, you will make work, so do what you want to make work."

I did not want a professional career over the opportunity to have a big family and be home with them. I wanted to work at making a home life with my sons and husband. Marc supported whatever I wanted. He did not want to be a "stay at home" dad, and we knew one of us had to stay home because we wanted more children. We both knew my sixty-hour workweek would never bring us happiness.

Marc and I had a great partnership despite the fact that we had our struggles and issues as every couple does. We will always look back on these years with young children as some of the best times of our lives even though we faced the challenges of balancing a crazy household, Marc's career, animals, diapers, temper tantrums, and our social lives.

We made sure to keep our marriage a priority. We always kept a list of goals we wanted to achieve. We called them "life contracts" and I remember how happy I was to see, "quality time with Marianne" as one of Marc's priorities. Our candlelight dinners, after the kids were put to bed, cut down on babysitting costs. Marc would tell the children that the best gift he could give his children was to "love their mother." I believe our kids benefited from the commitment we made to each other.

Journal Entry Father's Day 2002

I feel so lucky that my four children are growing up witnessing first hand how unselfish and sympathetic a man can be to others. My husband always puts himself last and makes sure everyone else is taken care of first. That's the role they are witnessing everyday in their father. What they do with that influence is now their choice. However I hope their father's passion to care for others comes through in their own lives and their own actions.

Whenever difficulties invaded our life, I would go through home videos and reconnect with what was important as I watched our lives unfold. In the old days, I would put highlights to music on a VHS tape and give them to Marc. I called them "gratitude" videos as I truly felt blessed with such a wonderful life. One night many years after our tragedy, Marc and I watched a VHS tape of Marc's thirty-fourth birthday. It showed baby ducklings born under a bush in our old yard in Exton, the boys helping their dad hammering and carrying siding, and the kids laughing on a four-wheeler with their dad at the wheel. As we watched, it seemed like we were these "other" people experiencing tremendous joy. It seemed unbelievable that the life Marc and I had built together could ever be at risk—because we lost a son? How could one tragedy cause another?

As grieving parents, we found it extremely difficult to console one another. Separately, we both shed years of tears, but we were unable to comfort each other even though we had a history of a close, loving relationship. The death of Matt brought a complicated new view of life. My husband found it difficult to be a family as the "hole" became even more prevalent when the five of us were together. This hole could never be fixed or filled in. Matt's absence was excruciating and so difficult to accept because in many ways, Matt was the life of our family. With his relentless energy and enthusiasm, he uplifted us. He had a gift to make us laugh. Afterward, the empty seat at the dinner table could never be avoided. When there are six seats at a table, the empty one cannot go unnoticed.

Marc and I developed our own methods of survival. When he became sad, he got busy. Six months after the accident, some people in Skaneateles asked Marc to run for mayor. When Marc told me, I was overwhelmed and shocked that he could function well enough to put a campaign together. My grieving, sorrowful husband was running for mayor? I did not want to lead such an effort, but I attended a few campaign meetings and, in a crazy way, the effort became a huge diversion for both of us. Marc faced a nearly impossible battle against a long-time resident and employee of the village, but he wanted to give voters another option. The campaign was hard fought, and a record number turned out to vote. My dad, his life partner, and Marc's mom came for the election, and a good friend, Kimball, hosted a dinner for all of us. Marc lost, but he knew that he would eventually enter public service.

This mayoral campaign helped get us through Matt's senior year while the media coverage about the car crash continued endlessly. In the meantime, Marc signed up to build anything for anyone. He put in our new kitchen, which was designed with his sister, Tina. I did not have the capability to take on such a project. They just told me to pick out the appliances. That alone nearly put me over the edge.

Marc would later install a new kitchen for his sister, a new window for a friend, and then disappeared for weekends to build a shed at our camp on Bloody Pond. I moved through my husband's busyness but still craved the absolute silence and beauty on the Skaneateles "point," writing in my journal and having coffee with friends. I was determined to digest all that had happened and maybe to make sense of it.

> May 8th, 2005
>
> I have not stopped thinking about you Matt for one second. I miss you terribly and want your confidence around me. However, I love your brothers and sister and father and I want to be happy for them. I want to make their life wonderful still. I pray the image of your face in my head brings me only joy and love and not pain. I want you in my heart always with peace, love and respect for the good deeds you accomplished in your seventeen years.

Soon after our tragedy, a neighbor came to visit. She spoke about having lost an older teenage sibling in a drowning. I asked what she remembered and if she could explain how a child feels when they lose a sibling. As young as she was, she could still relay this experience. "I remember being so excited about Christmas one year after my sister's death. I went to my mother and said, 'Mom, aren't you excited about Christmas?'" She can still remember her Mom's response. "No, I can't be excited about Christmas because I am so sad about your sister." My friend made me realize that we must go on for our other children despite our pain in order to give them hope, love, and joy.

I think about this comment often. How can the brokenhearted person go on for others? The complexities of our situation consumed our life. We had issues with our children, issues with alcohol, with teenagers, prison sentences, friends, society, and the desire to make a difference. We had no idea how difficult life would become.

While I wanted to immerse myself in conversations about DWI, underage drinking, and teenagers as one way of coping, my husband had no tolerance of such talk. He wanted it to stop while I wanted to speak at every high school, call every parent who lost a child, and obsess over every death, every accident, every DWI—every day. My own children became weary of my obsessions. It took years for me to learn to let go of the torch at times. Not necessarily to put it down forever, but to manage my way of grieving. It was killing us.

Journal Entry September 27th, 2006

I had a volatile week. The weekend brought Marc and I to our knees. I was fraught with anxiety as his grief gripped him in a death trap. He was so short and angry with all of us. He was totally overwhelmed with the house, the teenagers, the attitudes and it all stemmed from a TV interview I did for Channel 9. The one-hour special brought him back to two years ago, and all the tears, pain, and anguish returned.

As I spoke about Matthew on TV, they showed his video clips of the prom, fishing, and lacrosse. It broke our hearts to see the disappointment of our life once again. We both felt the old anxieties return, which makes us feel unfocused, unsociable, and miserable.

Lindsay defended her friends and their decisions to participate in underage drinking in a way, which brought Marc further to his breaking point. He reacted defensively with the possibility that our marriage may not survive. That just blew me away that he would ever consider the possibility that our marriage would not survive. It never enters my mind as a possibility. I just never ever think of anything but my life starting and ending with Marc.

Marc's comments about us not surviving frightened me, so I tried to go back to what I used to love. I started filming sports and my children. I made music videos for Lindsay's and Alex's graduations. I planned graduation parties; we fixed up our home. I tried to garden, visit good friends, and travel. Balance and a good frame of mind helped. Beauty and new surroundings helped also.

But I also had a secret life as I tried to keep my passions to myself when overcome with "fatal vision." I tried to keep my "DWI" life under wraps and not constantly share it with my family and friends. I went privately to talks at the Syracuse justice center every few weeks to address DWI offenders, leaving my torn-out heart at the door. I slipped out at night to attend talks on parenting and drug and alcohol education. To this day, my children have not seen the educational DWI video Marc and I participated in called "Consequence of No Consequences." My children had had enough of it. I would leave it to them to say when the time was right for a "Matt moment." Life needed me to focus on our family and our home. I tried to be a *normal* mom, whatever that is.

I worked on my heart night and day. I learned some unbelievable life lessons: That our hearts are not indestructible; that they can become crushed, lifeless, and hardened. Sadness and depression threaten our well-being. When one suffers, it is a constant battle to stay hopeful.

At the time of Matt's death, a good friend was going through a terrible divorce. She said, "Your pain is so much worse than mine." My reply: an emphatic "No! That's not true!" One cannot compare suffering. Pain is pain, and it is real, and it hurts. We all must deal with the shoes in which we walk. We don't get to swap the cards we are dealt. As much as we would give to change the course of our lives, we cannot. The sooner we learn to cope, the better.

I remember we were invited to a reunion in Pennsylvania with all our old friends from Exton. Three months before Matt's death, one of our good friends from the old group, Butch, had become a quadriplegic after a single-car crash. We were still dealing with the horrific news. Here was a man who worked out every day and played basketball with Marc every week. He would spend the rest of his life in a wheelchair, paralyzed from the chest down. It was unimaginable to Marc and me. We were nervous to see Butch for the first time since all our lives had been altered.

Many of us cried as Marc and Butch embraced. My heart felt crushed as Marc told Butch, "I would rather be you." Yes, that's the depth of heartache we were experiencing. "God, take me, but don't touch my children—*please!*" Once again we are reminded that we don't get to choose our suffering. It cannot be compared or chosen or bartered.

There were years of fallout and ripple effects from Matt's death. But nothing prepared me for year four. Despite the life purpose we had so actively pursued, Marc came to me and said he was unhappy. He was not sure how to overcome it. We sought a Christian counselor in the hope that we could move through our grief. The therapist listened and surmised we had both "overfunctioned" in seeking to overcome our grief. We seemed stuck and needed guidance. The therapist read from the Bible.

> And we boast in the hope of the glory of God. Not only so, but we also glory in our sufferings, because we know that suffering produces perseverance; perseverance, character; and character, hope. And hope does not put us to shame, because God's love has been poured out into our hearts through the Holy Spirit, who has been given to us.
>
> Romans: 5:1–5(NIV)

Once again, we were brought back to the concept of embracing suffering and accepting it as a way of life. Nothing would change our loss, but perhaps we could find a way to help each other through the worst moments. I asked my Christian friends to say a prayer for Marc and me. Then I propelled myself through the darkest period since Matt's death, seeking in scripture and Christian books rays of hope. I wondered whether our suffering was building character or breaking us apart. In weak moments, I was terrified.

During this difficult time, the summer of 2008, two friends sent us *The Shack* by William P. Young. I certainly felt that we were meant to read it. The book touched a strong nerve for both of us. In it, a father struggles with the murder of his young daughter. For many years, he is gripped with a "great sadness" that consumes his life. Marc and I understood this term and grabbed on to it, realizing our deep-rooted unhappiness now had a name and description. The main character in the book has a difficult time learning to love again.

His "great sadness" prevents him from moving forward in life. He remains stuck in his grief.

> Pain has a way of clipping our wings and keeping us from being able to fly, and if left unresolved you can almost forget that you were ever created to fly in the first place.
>
> —William P. Young
> *The Shack*[12]

Likewise, a human is born to love. But if the heart remains hardened too long, you are at risk of forgetting how. This author must have suffered in order to write such an eloquent book about loss and death.

It's no coincidence that this book was put before our hearts and that it helped us understand some of our complex emotions. I was fearful about our ability to love each other as we once did. The great sadness frightened me as we tried to unravel the complexities of our bereaved parenthood and marriage. It appeared that our unresolved grief was ripping us apart instead of making us into the "good new us."

After the painful summer of 2008, Marc and I ended up doing what we once loved doing the most—camping. I knew it would be a good idea to return to our roots and bond on a campsite in Lake George. The weekend was beautiful as we remembered how we once camped with our children on those islands. We picked a site with a beautiful view of sunrise and sunset from a big rock. We brought *The Shack* with us and read it together and apart. We digested the messages. We grieved together, and we discussed the changes in our lives and our marriage. We did a lot of healing and loving. I was encouraged that if we did the work, we could get through this.

A new statistic came out from the organization called Compassionate Friends regarding the true facts of bereaved parents and divorce. They cite the results of their survey from 2006.[13]

> Flying in the face of the conventional belief that couples who experience the death of a child are virtually destined to divorce, a survey released today finds that divorces among bereaved parents are far lower than that of the general public, and dramatically lower than is often portrayed by professionals, the media, and even those within the bereavement community.
>
> The survey shows a divorce rate of only 16 percent among bereaved parents, far below the 50 percent divorce rate usually cited for couples in general within the United States. Conducted earlier this year under direction of The Compassionate Friends, the nation's largest self-help bereavement organization for families that have experienced the death of a child, the survey confirmed the general findings of a 1999 study, also for The Compassionate Friends, that showed an even lower 12 percent divorce rate among bereaved parents.
>
> "This survey proves once and for all that the 70, 80, even 90 percent divorce rate so often quoted in the media, by professionals, and even the bereavement community is completely wrong," says Patricia Loder, executive director of The Compassionate Friends.
>
> "While the death of one's child definitely places stress on a marriage, we believe the divorce rate is so low because of the commitment parents have to survive their tragedy as a shared experience," says Mrs. Loder, who herself received a warning about the high divorce rate from a hospital nurse nearly sixteen years ago, following a car crash. "First I was told my children had died. Then I was told my marriage

would die. There are no words that can describe how that warning compounded the grief I already felt."

"It is now imperative that those of us within the bereavement community dispute this fictionalized 70 to 90 percent divorce rate whenever it surfaces," she says. "This myth must be laid to rest."

—The Compassionate Friends, 10/6/2006
http://www.compassionatefriends.org/CMSFiles/
X101206Press_Release_Survey,_Divorce-National.pdf

In 2010, our family watched the heartache of divorce. Two of our best friends separated, and our friendships would never be the same. We had gone on vacations with them, and our children viewed them like second parents. When we told our children of the breakup, they were crushed. It was a small glimpse of the pain that children endure when their own parents divorce.

Marriage is so important to our society. If I were to voice one ill of our country and society, it would be the failure of marriages. I watched my daughter suffer incredibly as she watched Marc and I struggle. It broke my heart to see how it affected her. Children are the victims of a broken marriage, and my heart aches that more marriages aren't saved through good Godly counseling. It takes work, but it can be done with will and love and faith. It's unfathomable to me to let almost thirty years of marriage and family end in failure.

I have watched many friends suffer from divorce, knowing that the pain is similar to death in that it requires years to heal. I understand also that the failure of marriage can result in destructive feelings, such as rejection, bitterness, and plummeting self-esteem. The sense of loss is horrific but far different from death. With death, you can still find a way to celebrate the marriage and the life you had together. With divorce, you want to destroy those memories because they are too painful to revisit.

I have witnessed too many times how the beautiful old marriage photos must suddenly be removed, but the pictured photos of a deceased loved one can hang forever on the wall and in the heart.

After years of trying to regain happiness together with our painful memories, I found a marital program called Retrouvaille. Retrouvaille is a type of marriage renewal for couples who are struggling. They are offered as weekend retreats around the world, run by couples who have been through the program. I found one close to our camp in Marathon and asked Marc if he would do the initial weekend. He agreed, so I signed us up for a weekend commitment of communication.

Marc wrote on the initial night of the program. "I guess our marriage has been in a state of flux for years, and it is exhausting. I hope this weekend, we can find some answers whether our struggle is worth it."

I attribute much of my personal healing to this program. It has been developed through years of marital experience and was founded on sound principles. Rule 1: A feeling is never right or wrong; it just is. The program is based on sharing feelings in order to understand each other better, to remove or soften resentment, and to learn to communicate so that resentments do not build.

I realized in that painful weekend that I was resentful of Marc. As much as I had tried to forgive him for his own methods of healing and grief, I had not come close to the understanding and forgiveness that he needed. The weekend involved hours and hours of communication via the written word and one-on-one discussion for building trust and commitment. The couples running the program shared deeply about their own relationships, encouraging conversation and healing for all of us. We both later realized that we felt better about our marriage and our future. We learned that the commitment to each other and our family was a choice for us to make. As much as some days we may not "feel it," we can choose to do it for the sake of our children, our future, and our potential happiness. We know we are better together. I know committing to our marriage was and is the right thing to do.

On the final evening of the program, the coordinators asked each of the couples to rise. They said, "All of your children are going to be so happy you are here trying to save a family."

Since Matt's death, Marc and I have suffered greatly, and our marriage took a big hit during some of these years. I know now how giving up can happen to the best of marriages. Pain can make one "crazy," as a therapist explained to us. Intolerable pain makes one feel totally helpless and willing to do anything to escape it. This includes withdrawing, isolating oneself, and feeling entitled to escape it any way possible.

Marc wrote an account of his "Five-Year Journey" so I could understand his grief.

> I am supposed to be strong, mentally tough, competitive, not exposing to anyone the emotional hell I live every day. I have had my moments of positive influence on the family I love so dearly. I have had my moments of careless selfish behavior that disappointed everyone but seemed to offer some relief, a distraction from reality.
>
> My journey has brought me away from so many people. Many were friends from my life before the tragedy. Realizing that insignificant conversations were meaningless, I avoided situations that I normally would have participated in. I attempted to create a new me, carefully selecting the people I knew I could share my grief with; those friends and family members that would give me a pass on being self indulgent and not working on the relationship, assuming they would just "understand." I depended on Matt's death to feel like I never had to "fit" in. I believe this process is wrong. I can still be me, sort of, just more sensitive.
>
> I don't want to burden anyone with my sorrow. When the "Great Sadness" comes, I feel a need to work it alone. I can't share it, at least I don't think I can. The "Great Sadness" is a feeling to total hopelessness. I can't find the light as I wallow in darkness of grief. I am afraid of this feeling. It is so un-natural to anything I have ever experienced. I have

always been able to work out any problem, mostly on my own; this seems insurmountable. I accept its defeat of my will. I look for it to pass or something to distract me when it comes. It may be depression, but I don't feel it all the time. It is more acute than chronic so I discount it as not being serious. I feel entitled to being depressed.

Entitlement is dangerous. I feel entitled to not participate in life at times, especially when others are enjoying themselves. I thought I would never laugh again soon after Matt died. But I found that to be untrue. I feel entitled to make mistakes with the excuse of losing a child. It is true that life at first was a constant struggle to continue. But that has somewhat subsided. I was told early on my marriage would fail also. That is what is expected, but I disagree with that way of thinking. Nothing has to really happen. I have to want it to happen. When I have felt frustration with my marriage, getting away from it helps me to realize that these feelings are temporary. I want my marriage to succeed and I want my family. I can't have any of it without my marriage. It is all tied together.

My pain drove me to do the opposite of Marc. I sought to share it, feeling the constant need to discuss it, analyze it, and make sense of it. Marc chose to be busy with constructive activities, such as running for mayor, becoming a village trustee, and building anything he could volunteer for. I did not want to be busy to avoid my pain. I wanted to go through it and get to know it. I wanted the pain to become my friend. I did not want to avoid it or fear it; I wanted to overcome it.

Many people could not grasp this angle of healing, including my own husband and children, at times. Nor could I grasp Marc's busyness. It took years and the Retrouvaille program to understand each other and to realize there are different ways of coping and healing. In the end, we may have landed together, but it took the utmost patience, love, and guidance. There were times we could have called it quits. We didn't. We continued to love each other, despite our brokenness. We sought help, we went away together, and we rekindled loving emotion. We spent time loving our three living children. Our family has meant everything to us, and we never wanted them to be disappointed that their parents didn't do everything possible to save the family and the marriage. I hope that our resolve can someday encourage our children to fight for their marriages.

I questioned my therapist recently about the years it took Marc and me to feel comfortable again. She said, "Sometimes, it just takes that long." However, I realize that time alone does not heal all wounds. Healing is a choice and does not happen solely by the passing of time. Healing can only happen through hard work and the desire to heal. I have heard people say we hold on to our grief because it represents our child, and if we let go of our grief, we let go of our child. I disagree with that. Matt will live on with us in all we do and experience.

As much as these words resonated with us, they were difficult to believe at times. We fought the "great sadness," and it appeared to beat us many times. It's an ongoing battle, but one we are better equipped to handle year after year. There is hope in this. This is my reason for wanting to share our pain. I am praying that somewhere out there, someone will live and love better as a result of our sharing.

Journal entry April 30th, 2011

I have such gratitude for this moment. Lord, I thank you for all your wisdom, discernment, and love for Marc and I. You have truly blessed our lives by giving us each other. We have tried to do your will always and are committing to our marriage and family. Thank you for giving us such strength to learn to live and love again.

My Faith Journey

Journal Entry August 27, 2004

I decided in a big way to develop my faith. I've gotten comfort in anything to do with God, faith, Holy Spirit, grace, Jesus Christ, the resurrection, the revelation, afterlife, forgiveness, love, and fellowship. Those are all good words and bring me hope and peace. If faith is not present I am in for deep trouble. I want to improve my relationship with God, knowing it only brings me closer to Matthew. I have never wanted to visit heaven more than I do right now.

Because I was raised Catholic and attended nine years of Catholic school, the Christian life is not foreign to me. I spent years learning about faith, grace, love, and sin. I received the sacrament of confirmation when I was in fifth grade, and I attended mass at the Newman Center at the University of Delaware. I was always a believer, never questioning the undying faith of my parents who gave generously to the Catholic Church in town. I believed in my heart "there is a God who knows us well and cares about us." I remember journaling as a teen to God, knowing he would always be there and would listen.

But all the background in the world does not prepare you for the step of faith you must take when you lose someone so dear. Faith is a choice to believe what you never see. I have made the decision to trust that Matt is now joyously a part of "eternal life" and that in time I will be with him again. We will be reunited in the next life—God's life. I now must learn patience and live this life as best as I can—without Matt's physical presence.

Churchgoing has been sporadic in my life. I went from attending daily mass back in eighth grade to rarely going as an adult, because I had four young children to dress and make behave. Nevertheless, Marc and I joined St. Mary's of the Lake parish when we moved to Skaneateles in 1996. All our children participated in religious education and received Holy Communion. Matt had just received the sacrament of confirmation during his sophomore year in 2003. As parents, we did our best to introduce all our children to faith and God.

We were fortunate to be members of St. Mary's at the time of Matt's death. The entire faith community turned out for our family, and we could feel the love and prayers from so many. I needed desperately some faithful people to reassure me of Matt's eternal life and to help us through this life-altering pain. Since we don't often think about death and what is truly needed in one's darkest hour, a church community can mobilize quickly to give grace and meaning to the end of a life. Father McGrath's homily helped me immensely and was powerful to everyone at Matt's funeral. It was later published in our local paper.[14]

> What does one say on an occasion like this? You have to allow me to ask that question of myself. One thing I don't say is something that will answer all of our questions. I don't have all the answers. The answers are written in eternal life. Someday, if we do what we are supposed to do, and follow God's will, those answers will unfold for us. But one thing is certain, a beautiful life has ended on this earth. And another thing is certain as well-that same beautiful life continues in eternity. And the loving God about whom we are going to speak in a minute or so, is waiting for that beautiful life to come and be apart of eternal life. Now, if we all had our way we would like to interrupt that process. Stop it. Turn it around. You know we don't have our way.
>
> —Father McGrath

After Matt's death, Marc and I frequently attended mass on Sundays. However, being in church brought images of Matt's coffin and the flowers that adorned the front of the church during the funeral. It was a bittersweet effort, fighting the pain of grieving for our son vs. wanting to be there to ask the Lord to care for him and us. For Marc, church often became a time of sorrow; but for me, new support systems developed.

I became close with one particular director of the church, Mary Gregory, who asked me one day to be a part of a new endeavor called "Renew," which would bring people together in small groups to share faith and life. This was a difficult time for me. I moved through the "yes" and attended the first meeting. I had just finished reading a book called the *Prayer of Jabez* by Bruce Wilkinson. Jabez, a very small character in the Bible, asks God to bless him and help him to enlarge his territory.

> And Jabez called on the God of Israel saying,
> "oh that You would bless me indeed,
> and enlarge my territory,
> that your hand would be with me
> And that You would keep me from evil,
> that I may not cause pain!"
> So God granted him what he requested.
>
> 1 Chronicles 4:9–10

I decided to pray the prayer of Jabez for myself. I pleaded, "God, help me to be comfortable doing these very uncomfortable things." Faith sharing? Actually telling how God is helping me through this horrific journey? Do I have the courage, confidence, and strength to share with such a group? *God, help me to enlarge my territory.*

Renew became a critical part of my healing. As the year unfolded, with opportunities to share Matt's story to large groups of teens and parents, my Renew group cheered me on. They gave me confidence and encouragement that I was doing the right thing. They supported me and seemed amazed by the changes going on in me.

To honor Matt's memory, I wanted to become a better person. I felt determined to beat the ripple effect of our loss. I knew that I felt my best on days that I actively loved and felt God's presence. I prayed for God to help me to be strong and understanding and forgiving. I longed for the days when the Holy Spirit was present and with me.

Who is this Holy Spirit and how can it help me? I read a book called *The Counselor* by A. W. Tozer. I suggested to my Renew group we devote time to this book and learn about the Holy Spirit. I was drawn to the concept of supernatural strength and the power of God because the healing going on in me seemed supernatural at times. I wanted to have the Holy Spirit around me more and more and experience the fruit of the Spirit which seemed to be a way of life that really worked.

> But the fruit of the sprit is love, joy, peace, forbearance, kindness, goodness, faithfulness, gentleness and self-control.
>
> Galatians 5:22 (NIV)

Who could argue over this way of life and having this kind of fruitfulness? The Holy Spirit is another sense besides hearing, touching, feeling, tasting, and seeing. It is a sixth sense of divine strength coming only from God. Tozer refers to the Holy Spirit as an Illuminator. He says, "The Holy Spirit can show us more of God in a moment than we can learn without Him in a lifetime."[15]

I learned that the Holy Spirit was given to us as our counselor to help us through all sorts of times. It was a gift from Jesus' death on the cross. The power of the Spirit is available to those who ask. As I kept learning about this beautiful Spirit, I became aware of the days which were full of the Spirit and those that grieved the Spirit. The days which were full of the Spirit were so much more peaceful for me. The days I felt unforgiving, angry, and resentful were my bad days of grieving the Holy Spirit.

Gradually, the Christian way started to make more sense to me and I could understand healing and faith because my heart was being changed daily. God changes your heart. The Christian way encourages you to share deeply with others, which helps you develop true relationships. I confirmed this to myself after years of reading Christian books, doing Bible studies, and surrounding myself with Christian friends. They represented true hope to me because they allowed me to share honestly and deeply. They were able to look at my face of suffering—without looking away.

When I moved to Skaneateles in 1996, I attended an informal Bible study in a new friend's kitchen. Nan Corsello, Steven's mother, was one of the women who studied with us. I started to learn about the Bible. Initial discussions with this group of women raised my curiosity further. The leader, Trudy Scarr, described to us her day of being born again in Christ. The concept was confusing to me because I was raised to believe in Jesus Christ, so I never had a life-altering moment of enlightenment. However, when she described a personal relationship with God through scripture and the Holy Spirit, it seemed like such a freeing concept to me. Faith was not about church rituals and rules; it's about getting to know God better through his word and having the Holy Spirit live inside of me. This was my day of reckoning. I finally understood deep down inside that church alone was not going to save me, but deepening my faith and being more "Christ like" would.

This small group of women, meeting in a kitchen weekly, eventually led to the establishment in Skaneateles of Community Bible Study, a worldwide organization educating people in God's word. I attended the first year of studies but soon allowed other commitments to take priority.

After Matt died, I wanted to start attending again, but I thought there was no room for two grieving moms. Steven's Mom, Nan, had been going, so I felt I needed to allow her to have this privilege without my uncomfortable presence. But by 2008, I desperately wanted to start attending because I needed structure in my faith. Thankfully, the organization was sensitive to the privacy needed for Nan and I to be in separate groups.

I have been attending CBS ever since. It grounds me weekly. And yes, now there is room in this wonderful group for Nan and me. I embrace Nan with love, and we share news of our children. We care about each other and about how our families are doing. We are true friends in Christ, and I love seeing her each week.

Each week, I leave with renewed faith and strength. CBS has the most amazing spiritual director who has a gift for breaking down this complicated book called the Bible. Using inspirational messages each week, she makes it meaningful for today's problems and questions

In my small group, I get an opportunity to occasionally speak about Matt and how faith is helping my grief. I also leave with the determination to work on my family and personal relationships. It has been instrumental in teaching me more about forgiveness. The most help, however, comes in learning about my priorities. Each week, I am encouraged to ask for God's help in knowing what his will is for my life. What is my purpose, oh, God, and how do you want me to accomplish it? I feel drawn to help others because of my nine years of trials and tribulations.

I also ask God to bless each of my opportunities to speak to students in high schools and to let me say the right words to touch hearts and change lives. Until I feel dismissed from this calling, I intend to carry on with messages of hope, love, and faith. However, I get weak and confused at times and need this weekly dose of strength to continue. As I make room for this Tuesday morning in my life, I know it will lead to more good things. Thank you, CBS, for being in my life.

Years ago when I grieved by Skaneateles Lake, I had asked the daunting question, "Where are you, Matt?" That's the question we all beg to know when someone is gone. Carol Kent, author of *A New Kind of Normal*, describes it as "eternity thinking." How do we trust in eternal life? The key to healing is developing a sense of trust and faith that this answer will reveal something beautiful, peaceful and pain relieving.

A pastor who spoke at CBS said that in order to trust someone, you must get to know him or her. This profound sentence applies to so many relationships in our lives, including spouses, children, friends, doctors, and God. To trust God and his plans for our children, we need to get to know him. That is my intent when I persistently educate myself in the Christian way. The more I get to know God, the more I trust his plans.

Recently, my sister asked me what we could possibly say to a young mother from Long Island who lost her three children in a car crash. A family member, driving under the influence, was responsible. I believe with all my heart and soul that we are put on this good earth to lean on each other and learn from each other. That is why there are books upon books, stories upon stories, and places to share easily and readily. That is why there is a Bible, a church, and a community center. We are meant to share and inspire each other, promoting hope, faith, and a reason to live.

As my heart ached for this young mother, I decided to write her a letter. I passed the letter on to my sister so she could forward it to mutual friends. The pain this woman and her husband were experiencing is incomprehensible. My husband expressed it in a meaningful way. "They would have to decide if their life is worth living." Would life be worth living after experiencing such a catastrophic loss? My answer is yes. This young couple will grieve, suffer, and have to take one day at a time—for a very long time. There is no timetable for the end to their suffering and heartache. Losing a child is the most sorrowful of life experiences, and losing all your children is unspeakable. But in my letter, I offered this hope to this young couple.

> This world needs you. Yes, our world needs people who suffer. The human race is dependent upon past sufferers to help us keep going. Suffering is such a different experience for so many on this planet. So many people never truly

comprehend what suffering is and may never experience a life altering degree of it. But many of us do suffer. Many members of the human race do not escape tragedy.

You have been given a burden so great that life may be too overwhelming to continue. However, the opportunity is there for you to survive in a way that you light the world with your determination and will to survive. We need you. We need you to show us that the human spirit can become so strong that a message of love and hope will prevail. So many people are praying for you and wanting you to be ok. It's an amazing world and the support for all of us who suffer is unlimited.

You have been given such a unique opportunity to prove to the entire human race that it can be done. Just like thousands of years ago in the Bible, just like Jesus and Paul, Job and Joseph, just like the endless families before you who have seen devastation, the human spirit can go beyond the normal existence of life, and live for some greater unknown purpose understanding that the sole will to live is being recorded by millions and used for the good of society. By sharing the will to live, you can inspire millions of fellow humans. It can be done. Someday you will be rewarded for your courage and strength. You may be rewarded in this life still; however, I do believe the true reward will be a beautiful reunion in eternal life with your beloved children. Take one day at a time, ask God to bless you, and offer up your suffering so others may be strengthened and encouraged that we, God's children, can survive anything with support from each other. There is hope for all of us. I am sure of this.

—Letter to Bereaved Parent

It is amazing to say that this couple recently had another child and the bereaved mother has since published a book called *I Will See You Again*. Without even knowing whether my letter ever got to her hands, I am so in awe that she was able to share her journey in the form of a book before me.

Angels and Coincidences

Albert Einstein said, "Coincidence is God's way of remaining anonymous." I believe we were given true angels from God to help us through this journey. It is very strange how the people you think will be there for you are not always the ones who are actually there for you. Some people just are not capable, but God will find others who are and send them to you as he did for Marc and me.

We were already acquaintances with a couple living in Skaneateles through our sons who were friends in school. I had no idea how close we would become after our loss. Mike and Meg arrived on our doorstep soon after the tragedy with true tools to help. Mike was a Christian therapist of twenty-five years, and Meg had the capability to discuss any type of pain and suffering. They already had experience helping couples who had lost children. The first day they showed up, Mike offered this advice: Try to practice HALT, do not be hungry, angry, lonely, or tired all at the same time. wow! Such simple advice but not always so obvious! These four feelings are so wearisome for an individual, but experiencing all four at the same time is exhausting. We began to realize that our breakdowns involved some of these factors. Marc and I spent years with Mike and Meg, seeking out their advice on many occasions. I apologized to Meg once about how needy we were and she emphatically responded with, "Mike and I find it a privilege to help you and Marc!" Despite how much our social lives had changed, we were blessed now with friends who knew how to embrace our pain—and who were not afraid of it.

In the first summer after Matt's death, Marc and I attended a "Hope for Bereaved" support group meeting in Syracuse. It was torture to feel the sorrow in that room. Marc likened it to a concentration camp, recognizing a certain "look" in all our faces. He vowed never to return to a room full of such pain. However, one kind woman who had lost her son in a hunting accident two years earlier gave me her phone number. A month later, I called. *What an angel!* Jeanette and I connected over coffee and developed a deep friendship, "sharing our stones" for the last nine years. Amazing! The connection you can make with a fellow sufferer can be unique and uplifting. This is why a group such as Hope for Bereaved is crucial to every community. When you walk in the door, you are greeted by someone who understands your pain and who is willing to listen and offer empathy that most people find difficult to give.

I was asked to interview Jeanette recently about how the organization helped her. On the tenth anniversary of her son Ben's death, we travelled to our camp and set up the video equipment. We laughed and cried, as we sat in front of our new fireplace, and we pondered healing. "Yes," she said, "I met some great friends at Hope who helped me in the journey. They get it. I am not going crazy. I am just grieving." Thank you, Jeanette, for sharing your stones with me—and taking so many of mine!

During his freshman and sophomore years, Marc and I had encouraged Matthew to enter the confirmation program at St. Mary's Church. This was a huge commitment in Skaneateles because the church is extremely strict and accepts no excuses for missing sessions of religious education. At first I worried that Matt wouldn't take the program seriously. His stated reason for committing to it: "It will be good to have if I marry a Catholic girl." Another complication was that Matthew needed to find a mentor. For most, this meant an aunt or uncle. But we had no family in the area, and most close friends either were not available or not Catholic. Finally, Matt decided to accept a volunteer from the church. I was surprised, saying, "Are you sure you want to be assigned just anybody?" He replied, "Yes, maybe they will become a good friend."

Once again, some things are just not accidental. Matt was assigned a Christian neighbor who lived just a few houses away. For two years, Matthew periodically walked down the street for mentor time with Jack Haggerty. The two studied all aspects of Christianity and Catholicism. Jack later shared with me his workbook, which encouraged conversations about all walks of life, including afterlife. For Christmas, Jack gave Matt a book called *20 Essential Rules of Life*. I remember reading it after Matt and highlighting it so I could remember some of the messages. Jack was a pilot. He looked forward to taking Matt up in his plane and sharing their love of flying.

Matt's death crushed him. At the wake, after standing in a long line in the church, Jack handed Marc and I his "wings." To this day we have them safely tucked inside Matt's cabinet, beside the American Flag. I am forever grateful that such a devout Christian man mentored Matt. Though teenagers rarely embrace the church, a deep profound faith can develop from knowing people of great faith. I believe Matt was well prepared for God's embrace.

More "angels" of support arose through our families who were extremely supportive throughout our tragedy, providing help with our children and in our home. But we observed the same truth; there were those who could talk and interact about the tragedy, and there were those who just could not handle painful conversations.

My sister Susan was blessed with a true spiritual gift. She embraced my pain, listened persistently, and constantly encouraged me to continue helping, sharing, and getting to know God. Susan became my spiritual mentor, leading me along a path of healing and transformation. I found a source of joy in life along with strength to endure fear and the unknown. At times, my future seemed unclear and insecure, and the anxiety became unbearable. But Susan showed me positive ways to deal with it. She encouraged faith and patience. She was a lifeline, and I am forever grateful for her daily walk with me.

I had an amazing relationship with my parents throughout my life. From high school sports to college parties and regular visits to the grandchildren, my parents were threaded throughout my life. I grew up with the benefit of two parents who adored each other and who were committed to all six children. I enjoyed their company and wanted to share them with friends in all walks of life.

In high school, I would make sure they were home to be at my parties. In my married life, my dad could be counted on to entertain ten women, holding court in my home with a pot of coffee. When he arrived for a visit, he would immediately ask, "When are the girls coming to see me?" A bad word did not exist between my parents and me. I was fortunate.

The month before my mother passed away unexpectedly from a stroke at age seventy-eight, I interviewed my parents on the back deck of our house. They told their beautiful love story, from the teenage years when Dad would take Mom's back wheel from her bike so she couldn't pedal home. They hung out with the same gang in the Bronx and spoke with the famous accent that would never leave. My dad survived an alcoholic dysfunctional father, the Great Depression, and being shot down in a B-17 over Germany in World War II at age nineteen. He was an only child, hoping to have a big loving family. He got one! Matthew and all my children adored and admired my dad. There are so many high school biographies written about my dad by many of his grandchildren. One exists by Matt that was created over a conversation at a campfire at Bloody Pond in 2003.

Before Matt's death, my father and I were discovering a new relationship following the death of his beloved wife of almost sixty years. He was mourning deeply and had a sadness about him. I was trying to pick him up, to divert him with frequent visits to Skaneateles. After Matt's death, he and I were just lost together. I remember wanting to hide my pain from him but couldn't pretend to be the bright and shining daughter who brought happiness to his life. I was in a state of despair, and we clearly could not handle all this sadness between the two of us.

I found it difficult to face him in the early mornings when we talked and shared the newspaper. Now I wanted to run away and be alone.

In the summer of 2005, my dad found a special old friend with whom to share his life. He brought "the other Marianne," or "TWW (the widow Woodruff) as he often called her, to Skaneateles. Marianne brought a positive attitude and an uplifting spirit with her. She was a gift to my dad, and she rescued our relationship. Marianne could embrace our pain and talk openly about sorrow and tragedy. Years before, she had lost her husband and then a grandchild in a terrible accident. Thus she could relate to the long journey we faced. What a gift to my dad and me! We ended up sharing life, vacations, meals, and Skaneateles for almost three years. She helped us heal in so many ways and added a wonderful bond between my dad and me. I was fortunate to recognize early on the enrichment that a substitute mom can be. Marianne offered the most profound bit of advice to me. "Life is not about how smart you are or how strong you are. The secret to happiness is how you are willing to accept change." Marianne would later always describe each new challenge in her life as a "chapter" to embrace. She encouraged me to appreciate all the chapters as they would come.

Meanwhile, Marc remained at a loss to connect with his mother. He once came to me and said, "My mom has never asked me how I am." It broke my heart that mother and son could not share the loss of Matt. Marc's mom suffered silently and never spoke a word of grief to either Marc or me. It was sad to see this disconnection between mother and son. Neither could know nor understand how badly the other was hurting.

The first Christmas without Matt, we heard that Marc's mom had sent out a letter, telling everyone her grandson had died. We never received a copy. Who would know that she was suffering so much and needed to tell the world? It would be years before Marc could connect with her. She had suffered mini strokes and was facing a failing memory. Nearly six years after our tragedy, I encouraged him to talk with her during an upcoming visit. The time was right for the son to relay his hardships to his mother. I hoped a new bond would form. He said later after they finally shared, "I felt like she was my mom again."

Yes, to be truly connected to each other, we must share. Where there is true sharing, there is a true bond. It is never too late.

Matt's Spirit

One year after Matt's death, my friend, Lori Ruhlman, editor of the Skaneateles school newspaper, summed up the message of a therapist who spoke on spirituality at Skaneateles High School.

> Connect with something out there that is "greater than you." Some people do this through religion or spiritually. It is helpful to know that something remains. The spirit remains. Connect with the best of that spirit of the person who is gone. Try to live that out in honor of that person. They continue to live through you on that level.

Around Skaneateles, the tributes to Matt and his spirit are everywhere. I know Matt's Mass card with his picture is sitting on many dashboards. A neighbor designed stickers displaying the initials "MA," Matt's handle. The stickers can be seen on cars here and there. You can still find it inscribed into a few sidewalks around town. As soon as the cement was poured, he managed to get his initials down. One is in front of the Sherwood Inn where he worked.

Matt's memory also lives in three trees planted around the village. One is a beautiful apple blossom that graces the entrance to the high school and the others are by the lake that we both loved so much.

People paid their respects in their own individual ways. My brother-in-law made a rocket with the initials MA and fired it thousands of feet into the sky as hundreds of onlookers cheered. Matt's lacrosse coach designed a lacrosse T-shirt with Matt's number 9. The first Thanksgiving after the tragedy, Pete Torrey, a friend of Matt's, came to our house to sing a song he wrote, called "A Perfect State of Mind." It was beautiful. He sang of angels, saying, "Another one's been cut down...It took this town two weeks just to come back to life." I used this song in Matt's video.

A high school memorial fund raised over $25,000 and included a fundraiser by Marc's family down at the Jersey Shore. Marc's brother, Gregg, raised the majority of the money with a race. The high school then purchased weight equipment and hung a lacrosse photo of Matt in the weight room where generations of youngsters will work out.

In a cabinet of our family room, a folded flag accompanies Matt's Air Force photos. A quilt of his faded, worn T-shirts drapes his bed and my assembly tables. The list can go on and on, but know this—the greatest tribute to Matt is the heightened awareness his story brings.

Journal Entry
11/1/05
At the Aurora Inn

Yesterday Marc and I woke with heavy hearts. He had a dream about Matthew last night who appeared at the front door and was only about eight years old.

I so remember that age as we had just moved to Skaneateles. He was learning to skate and used to practice skiing down the driveway. He loved the snow and to build jumps and forts. He had a huge K'NEX project of a booby trap in the basement, which he and Alex worked on forever while we unpacked boxes. He needed friends so bad and made them quickly in school. He loved the cabin, our dog Gretchen, and his snake, an albino corn snake called "Checkers."

Marc said that in the dream Matt wanted to help me with my videos. That just hit me as so real because the last dinner I had with him he told me he loved my business. It's almost like he is watching me work and is helping me along the way.

Matthew, I hope you are happy and not too sad for us. I told Dad this morning, "Did you realize how much we love you? Did you realize how much we miss you?" The depths of our love for you, and for all of our children, is a new deeper depth beyond any comprehension.

The summer of 2005, one year after Matt's death, focused great attention on similar tragedies across upstate New York. The police chief in DeWitt, Eugene Conway, created a traveling exhibit called "Gone4ever" to show the young lives lost in the Syracuse area. The exhibit featured images and stories of three separate car crashes taking the lives of five students and sending three drivers to jail for excessive speeding or driving while intoxicated. I was asked to contribute some of Matt's belongings to the memorial. A kind woman came to my home where I had spread out Matt's awards, lacrosse gloves, jerseys, photos, and other personal belongings on the dining room table. This was one of the most painful exchanges. The woman sensed my emotions and acknowledged how difficult this was to do. How surreal to be giving your son's belongings to travel in an exhibit on children who have died.

At the time, I needed to be assured that I would someday get everything back. But now, I rarely think about those material items. I don't miss them, and I believe they did a lot more good traveling to high schools than they would have sitting in my house. Eventually, "Gone4ever" was retired, as they all are. I remain eternally grateful to this brave committee of volunteers who organized the exhibit. The committee recently wrote to our family,

Since it was first unveiled in June of 2006, the *Gone4ever* exhibit has traveled to more than 140 schools in nine counties throughout Central New York as well as many other venues.

I truly believe that it has reached its objectives, and that it has altered at least one person's decision and thus prevented a further tragedy. It would not have been possible without the many contributions and contributors who helped make it happen, none-more than you.

—Gone4ever Committee

We were also blessed with endless tributes to Matt in the press. Matt's story has been told many times, so often that I assembled a website in his name (matthewangelillo.com). The site organizes the many published articles, family thoughts, essays, videos, and photos that honor Matt's life. One particular friend of Matt's, Dan Hunt, was interviewed several years later for a beautiful article written by a peer who had graduated from Syracuse University in 2009. Michael Bonner of the *Auburn Citizen* newspaper eloquently portrayed Dan's love for Matt and how he honors Matt's memory by wearing number 9 on the Wells College lacrosse field. As a former teammate, Dan Hunt took Matt's death very hard but has tried to live his life with courage and commitment to honor his good friend. A video interview produced by Bonner is displayed on Matt's website. Bonner writes,

The night of the accident, Hunt talked to Angelillo by phone and told him to be safe. Told him to not get in the car with anyone who couldn't drive. He told him he had a great life ahead of him.

It's words that are uttered millions upon millions of times from friends to friends, parents to children, and siblings to siblings. Hunt was knocked down for years, as the thought of what could have been lingered in his mind. He should have tried harder.

Dan says, "It's one way to outwardly express what he meant to me. It's a way of making his legacy not end. It's like he worked hard, so I'm going to work hard. He wore number 9, so I'm going to wear 9. This is the kind of stuff he stood for—teamwork, hard work. That's what I'm going to do. I'm not going to be one of those kids who doesn't have a plan. I'm not going to be a kid who wants to blend in. I don't want to blend in."

—Auburn Citizen, 5/31/10[16]

In July of 2012, I photographed Dan and Kim Hunt's wedding. It was a special day for all of us. Dan continues to be the friend who knocks on my door every year on June 19th. I am eternally grateful for this connection to Matt's life.

Clueless Video

One year after Matt's death, an organization called Prevention Network entered my world. In 2005, Phil Rose, coordinator of the "Underage Drinking Initiative" at Prevention Network in Syracuse gave a "shout-out" to the community, asking for people to brainstorm over the issue of teens and their alcohol use. This was my first involvement with Prevention Network. A committee of educators, law enforcement, drug rehabilitation facilities, a school superintendent, guidance counselors, professional prevention counselors, and parents met for two years. We shared a mutual consensus that real change must start with the parents. Recognizing the difficulty of getting parents to attend evening presentations, we sought a tool for when they are a 'captive audience.' The goal was a video to show during school orientations and appropriate events. A national authority on the issue, Milton Creagh, had come to Syracuse and pleaded, "Parents, you cannot afford to be clueless!" His words became the title for our video, *Parents, You Can't Afford to Be Clueless.*

Dozens of interviews were done with students and adults throughout the area. A group of us canvassed volunteers to discuss personal or professional experiences. I invited several people from Skaneateles, including Steven Corsello's pastor, Craig Lindsay, to tell how drinking had affected the community. At the time, Steven had just been released from state prison. I said to Pastor Lindsay, "If he would like to be in the video, we would love to include him." Phil reached out and Steven agreed—was even pleased to take part.

The video included a sheriff, a district attorney, an emergency room physician, a social worker, a professor at Syracuse University, and many parents and students affected by underage drinking. Steven's interview was incredibly powerful. He looked so hand-some, and his sensitive words struck a chord. "I will live with the accident until they put me in the ground," he said. "That never goes away." Copies of the video were sent to every middle school and high school in Onondaga County with the help of money from Matt's memorial fund at Skaneateles High School. *You Can't Afford to be Clueless: Raising Parent Awareness about Underage Drinking and Drug Use* was called "hard hitting, honest and helpful."

I wrote a guest column for our local paper to introduce the video.

> My own personal experience of losing my beloved son, Matthew, leads me to be involved in this project. "Hope for Bereaved" in Syracuse, teaches many of us to actively share our pain in the hopes of helping others and ourselves. I commend so many of the participants in this video as I know it is not easy to be public about our experiences. The most challenging task of the last two years was asking people to do such a thing…*share pain*. I thank every one of the participants in this video, as they will make a difference for so many others.[17]

> —Skaneateles Journal
> September 2008

Since the fall of 2008, the video has become a formidable tool for parents and educators across Central New York. In Skaneateles, it was used for high school and middle school orientations, and I personally presented it to a few health classes.

Consequence of No Consequences

Another video that told Matt's story came out at the New York state level under the STOP DWI program. Justice Centers across the country, or jails, as we know them, attempt to educate DWI offenders. One piece of the process is to bring in victims to share our stories during Victim Impact Panels (VIP), which are held every other week in cities across the state. Denis Foley, a coordinator of Stop DWI in Albany, asked Marc and I to participate in a video, which could be used for VIP education. Denis, involved in DWI prevention for many years, wrote a book in 1986 called *Stop DWI* in which he says, "Community prevention refers to the process whereby the public begins to prevent drunk driving in their immediate social circles, a process in which drinking and driving develops into a taboo behavior."[18]

> One element often is an incident so shocking and out of the ordinary that it shakes a community and holds it's attention. Thus, the symbol of a family shattered by the tragic example of a needless death violates not only the family but also the community. The infraction can affect society as a whole.
>
> —Denis Foley
> *STOP DWI*

In the summer of 2008, Denis used our family as such a symbol. Videographers showed up with Denis and set up a makeshift studio in our garage. Along with Marc and me, two of Matt's friends agreed to be interviewed. The video was titled *Consequence of No Consequences*, after Marc's statement in the courtroom.

Denis produced the video to accompany an exhibit called, "One Second Everything Changes" which travels extensively throughout New York. I've met educators all over the state who

213

use the video. They express enthusiasm about its impact. It's amazing how many people spread Matt's story, but I am grateful that I do not have to be personally involved with every sharing. The videos and exhibits educate by themselves.

Honor the Code

Eventually those of us who had been working together began to turn our attention to athletes, a group in which I was particularly interested since Matt and all my children were avid athletes. I had spent thousands of hours over my lifetime as a parent dedicated to my kids' teams, cooking up team dinners, videotaping games, making end-of-year highlight DVDs, and driving in bitter winter storms to attend all of their various games. I truly loved their teammates who could be found in our house at all hours of the day and night, and I felt very troubled over the use of alcohol I witnessed or heard about.

After years of striving to be an involved and aware parent of a teenager, I let my daughter loose in the world of college athletics. Ironically, Lindsay's Facebook page for her first semester at the University of Binghamton was filled with photos of "red cups" and social gatherings. Lindsay was recruited for lacrosse, which has been called the number one party sport by the American Athletic Institute. But the sport also recruits some of the hardworking athletes across our country. Lindsay ran miles every day, all summer, preparing for an endurance test called "the gauntlet." Her friends are also outstanding athletes on scholarships with great potential and personal drive. Yet the initial weekends at college involved drinking. Despite the fact that the American Athletic Institute's research shows that "one night of drinking negates fourteen days of training," a fact Prevention Network has used as a slogan for posters in high schools across Syracuse; the message too often falls on deaf ears.

So in 2009, Prevention Network went back to the drawing board to brainstorm the next wave of prevention in Syracuse. A committee headed by Phil Rose discussed ideas for a student message. We were inspired by a recent speaker in our community, Dr. Dennis Embry, who recommended that we stop paying so much attention to negative behavior and start focusing on positives. For Phil and me, it was as if a light bulb just went on in our minds. We said, "Let's reward those students who make good choices. Let's find a way to recognize them and use them to educate others."

At the same time I was asked by Denis Foley to participate in another DWI video aimed at athletes, which would be titled, *Living the Code*. Denis asked me to help highlight the devastation of substance abuse among athletes. A team of videographers gathered in the weight room at Skaneateles High School where Matt's dedication took place five years earlier and where his lacrosse photo hangs on the wall outside the trainer's office. There we interviewed Matt's football and lacrosse coaches. It was heart wrenching to hear them tell of Matt's death. Steven's coach added his important story too. In my heart I felt it was meant to come together in this room where all my children spent much of their athletic years. Prevention groups were targeting the athletic world. How appropriate, given that the news focused on so much destructive behavior in professional and college athletics. Every day, it seemed as though some athlete was charged with a crime related to drugs or alcohol. In 2011, a cover article in *Sports Illustrated* highlighted the high percentage of college football players with criminal records.[19] All signs pointed toward the need to educate athletes who are glorified in school and society for their athletic prowess.

A national speaker, John Underwood, who had appeared at the county's underage drinking summit, further inspired our committee. John works with the American Athletic Institute and has done extensive research on the effects of alcohol and other drugs. He travels far and wide for a program called "Life of an Athlete." He says, "If you don't teach kids a lifestyle, they will make one up." Often, the ones being made up include drugs and alcohol. His message is all-inclusive: mind, body and spirit are essential to become the best you can be. He has an extensive training program and then offers research and powerpoints free to everyone. His goal is to make our athletes, who are role models in society, healthy and successful. He encourages student athletes to lead the cause in their schools.

The other influential person in an athlete's life is the coach. Underwood said, "A student athlete probably spends more time with their coach than with their parents… So wouldn't you want their coach to have the same values as you?" Underwood stresses the need for coaches to be on board with the athletic code. He calls them "coaches who care to confront." The code must be enforced to give consequences to "out of bound" behavior. If no one enforces it, the school is permitting it. "Permit and you then promote."

Lindsay had very influential coaches in her life. Her high school lacrosse coach was adamant about the athletic code. Lindsay said, "No one would ever break the code on that team." Lindsay agreed there was less negative peer influence because the team came together to *honor the code.*

In 2011, a committee, headed by Phil Rose of Prevention Network, created a pilot program for high schools called "Honor the Code." It uses many of Underwood's messages. After meeting with several superintendents and athletic directors, we found four schools in our area – Skaneateles, Marcellus, Lafayette and Onondaga–interested in taking the program to their athletic departments. The athletic directors would market an athletic code under a new set of strategies and guidelines. "Honor the Code" is a partnership between coach, athlete, parent, team and school. It is proposed as a code of conduct, a way of life that reinforces individual responsibility and accountability to a school and a team. Honor the code and you honor your team, your coach, your school, your family and yourself. The committee including the student athletes, came up with a logo, poster and subheading, "It's what happens between games."

Peer pressure or as Underwood calls it, "peer influence" is a part of every high school student's life. So, why not make *not* to drink stronger than drinking? As Malcolm Gladwell states in the book *Tipping Point*, "Ideas and products and messages and behaviors spread like viruses do." The partnership of four committed schools is just a start. The concept is "power in numbers."

We began with the concept that student athletes from every school are leaders. Initially, a female and a male athlete were selected to take the program back to his or her school. We spent the first meeting with these students, educating them on our program and how they can help. That meeting was an eye-opener, as we asked them to discuss their own perceptions of the drinking that goes on in their schools. Each student said the athletic code was broken frequently and meant little to many students. They said, "It is something you sign and rarely read or understand." They said, "many do not take it seriously." Drinking goes on at every level regardless of whether one is a team leader or not. The students clearly expressed at this initial meeting that to be a drinker brings status; to abstain does not. The older athletes are leading the younger athletes to follow suit. It goes on everywhere. Honor the Code aims to change this perception.

A few months into the pilot program, I interviewed two students on the "Honor the Code" team. I asked what motivated them to not drink. One answer became clear: Both had strong role models. They were not easily influenced by peers and remained focused on their goals. They both had clear expectations of what they sought to accomplish, and they would let nothing get in their way.

One student mentioned two women—her mom and sister—whom she never wants to disappoint. She said her mother has always been a role model when it comes to drinking. She won't drink in front of teens and makes clear her disapproval of underage drinking. This student clearly benefits from strong parental influence and clear concise messages.

Recently, I had the opportunity to attend one of Underwood's leadership conferences for his "Life of an Athlete" program. This gave me access to other students leading efforts at their schools across the country. The message that comes across so clear and strong for students is "power in numbers" and not being *alone*. No student or adult wants to be alone in life. To just say, "I don't do that stuff" is not enough. But giving students a label with respect and honor gives other athletes facing similar choices someone with which to identify. It gives those who "Honor the Code" strength and courage to make a better choice about alcohol while at the same time fitting in with the other athletes.

One of our student leaders from Skaneateles wrote about his role in *Honor the Code* for the theme to his college essay. Bryce Kerr writes,

> The *Honor the Code* program utilizes a different type of leadership role for the representatives by asking them to educate their fellow athletes about the effects of substance abuse on athletic performance. I have welcomed the challenge, as a student, of communicating the program's objectives to my peers. I have discussed the issue at parent meetings, coaches meetings, and assemblies, as well as individually meeting with several teams. To raise awareness, we have brought guest speakers into schools, provided *Honor the Code* shirts and bracelets to Varsity student athletes, and have organized informational assemblies.
>
> This whole experience has been very rewarding for me. I believe that I have become an asset to this important and influential program, of which, only a handful of student-athletes in the country take part in. I have made it my goal to help prevent student-athletes from partaking in the consumption of drugs, alcohol, or tobacco products; furthermore, to help avoid the negative consequences that have come with their use/abuse.
>
> —Bryce Kerr
> College Essay, Skaneateles High School

At the end of our pilot year of *Honor the Code*, Prevention Network hosted a banquet for the teen leaders to reward their efforts. The athletes were commended for their courage and commitment. As I thought about how I would express my own gratitude to these athletes, I came across my first letter to the Post Standard, written after Matt died.

> So, what do we do? Let's start with finding some responsible teenagers out there to lead by example. There has to be some in every class who can be utilized to mentor others and clearly demonstrate that fun can be had without alcohol...Also, if they have goals and dreams... assure them how easy all the dreams in the world will be lost with one second of bad judgment. Let's keep talking...
>
> —Marianne Angelillo
> It Didn't Work [20]
> *Post Standard* 2005

I told the students, "It may have taken eight years, but I thank each one of you for being the leader that you are."

Prevention Network in Syracuse has been tireless in its work. Every time I get the opportunity to work with this amazing organization, I feel validated that this is where I should be in honoring my son. Phil Rose has been an incredible inspiration to me as he leads the community along with groups of teens to "question" underage drinking and to *honor the code*.

In one of my assemblies in my hometown of Florham Park, New Jersey, Brian Shottenheimer, who was at the time the offensive coordinator of the New York Jets, sat in the audience with his wife. I shared with him the concepts behind the *Honor the Code* program and said, "We will be giving you better athletes." Shottenheimer responded, "No, you will be giving us better people."

It's Up to Us

For the past few years, I have been asked to give closing remarks to fifth graders in Skaneateles who graduate from a program called STARS, "*s*tudents who *t*hink and *a*ct *r*esponsibly *s*ucceed." I would look out to these precious faces knowing they are in such an innocent, simple time of their lives. They came to graduation clearly planning to never abuse drugs or alcohol. Their parents were so relaxed, still feeling in control because they have spent years teaching their children values and responsibilities in an effort to protect them and keep them out of harm's way. Then I thought of my family's pain over losing Matt. I could picture him clearly in the fifth grade. I found a photo of him that year making a presentation to his fifth grade class. He loved his life, his school, and his family. He embraced all the assemblies that warned about drug abuse. He vowed to never smoke marijuana. He had hopes and dreams. He had so much fun with his friends.

Journal
Matt's letter to Dad in fourth grade with Mrs. Taylor

Dear dad,

You are going to be mad at me for something I did. It started this morning. When I was getting my morning drink, the fridge fell over and it made a hole in the floor and got smashed to pieces. That's just the beginning. When I was riding my bike to school it fell apart and I had to walk my bike to school. When I got home two kids were playing a joke on me and they set a cherry bomb off on my house. Luckily I got out of my house. I need some money. $500,000. Well bye,

Love Matt

And his dad's response:

Dear Matthew,

You do have a problem, however not as bad as you think. We can fix a hole in the kitchen floor. We can buy a new refrigerator. I can fix your bike, and the cherry bomb was really a bad dangerous joke. But you know what…no, big deal! You'll find the only thing I worry about is you being sick or ill. Everything else we can handle.

Those things that you mentioned are "material things" and once you have them you can figure out how to get them again. But I can't ever replace you so take care of yourself. I love you.

Dad

—Matthew Angelillo
Fourth Grade journal

Then my mind jumped to the statistics. Many of these students would experiment with drugs or alcohol in high school. Some would start in middle school. I thought of all the wonderful families I know who have suffered because of drugs and alcohol, who had their own unique losses. Were these fifth grade parents prepared to handle the changes that would inevitably come? What can we do to help? What could I tell these fifth graders and their parents?

I began by describing how hard our society attempts to solve medical problems and cure diseases so people can live long lives. We are not satisfied to bury an eighty-four-year-old. We want our parents and grandparents to live longer. So we have this incredible ability, as humans, to cure cancers, to create vaccines, and to do heart and lung transplants. But as smart as we are, we cannot cure the leading cause of death for adolescents between the ages of eighteen and twenty-four: accidents that more often than not stem from drugs or alcohol. Our society sends over 230,000 teens to emergency rooms each year alone! (SAMHSA – US Government study 2010)[21]

Teenagers are meant to test the world—along with their parents. Losing a child does not have to involve death. We can lose our children in other painful ways—alienation due to disagreements, personality differences, the child's need for independence, flat-out rejection of the parents—whatever the reason, the loss is real, it's frightening, and it hurts. Alcohol and other drugs are a real threat to a teenager's well-being and quality of life. They can sabotage relationships permanently in the best of families because temptations present themselves at the very time of life when teens and preteens are the most vulnerable. Middle school can be a "perfect storm."

Dr. Michael Riera[22] paints the life circumstances that can give rise to the Perfect Storm in his book, *Uncommon Sense for Parents of Teenagers*. Up until middle school, kids are comfortable with parents managing most aspects of their lives. Parents help choose friends, activities, and sports. They are chaperones, chauffeurs, or coaches actively involved with all aspects of their child's lives. Marc had coached all our children at this age. We were involved with families of friends, holding picnics, sports gatherings, and birthday parties. But in middle school, everything starts to change. The parent loses some control, and the child takes on more freedom and responsibility. They decide what academics subjects they like, whether they want to play sports or be involved in music, drama, community service, and most important of all, whom they want to hang out with and whom they will allow to influence their choices. The parent now becomes more like a consultant and loses the daily contact they had in elementary school. Teens now have their own private thoughts and behavior that is often hidden from their parents. At the very moment they are moving toward independence, scientific research tells us that the human brain is not fully developed until the early to mid-twenties. The underdeveloped frontal lobe is vulnerable to gaps in "problem solving." It falls prone to risky behavior especially in the teenage years. Add drugs or alcohol to the equation, and a "perfect storm" results because alcohol affects the decision-making area of the brain, exactly the area that is underdeveloped. It's a double whammy. *When you drink, you don't think.* Wisdom is completely compromised.[23]

> Wisdom is essential to have a good life...wisdom means having clear understanding and insight. It's discerning what is right and wrong...it's having good judgment...it's being able to sense you are getting too close to the edge. It's making the right choice or decision. We have no idea how many times simple wisdom has saved our lives or kept us out of harm's way or how many times it will continue to do so in the future.
>
> —Stormie O'Martian
> *The Power of a Praying Woman*

The key phrase here is "having clear understanding and insight." In the end, although Matt was intelligent, motivated, and very independent as a high school junior, he made a fatal choice because his own judgment or "wisdom" about not riding with a drunken driver was completely clouded because of the influence of alcohol on his brain. He lost his life in the "perfect storm."

But why do teens choose to use alcohol during these risky years? I believe it is because we live in a culture that condones and encourages the use of alcohol. Before our tragedy, Marc and I were unconscious about the pervasive use of alcohol all around. But in the past nine years, I have been challenged over and over with uncomfortable situations involving alcohol. High school graduation parties represented an oxymoron with their kegs, wine, and adults freely drinking in front of teenagers. We tell our teens to restrain from drinking, but yet we are showing them by example that drinking is part of the accepted social fabric, giving the not-so-subtle message that alcohol equals "having fun." Concerts are another venue where alcohol and drugs flow freely with no consequence. In 2008 when I took Lindsay to a Dave Matthews' concert because I love his music too, I was acutely aware of the number of inebriated and high teens who packed the show. Clearly, alcohol and drugs served as a prerequisite for many to have fun at a concert. As much as I love all types of music, I am mystified that pop artists often glorify alcohol in their music. All the education in the world cannot erase what our teens absorb from the world acting out around them.

Jean Kinney uses a simple scenario in her book, *Loosening the Grip: A Handbook of Alcohol Information*, to drive home some statistics about how our society drinks. If there are ten beers and ten people, three will not drink at all, five will share two beers, and two will drink eight. In other words, 30 percent of society does not drink, approximately 50 percent are social drinkers consuming 20 percent of the alcohol, and 20 percent will have a tendency to binge, consuming over 80 percent of all alcohol. I have used this example in assemblies for high school students, explaining that the two out of ten bingers cause most of the pain for everyone else. I told my daughter, Lindsay, that as much as kids think drinking in college is innocent, two out of ten may find themselves developing a dependency on alcohol. This holds true for adults, but the trend is worsening for college students. The latest statistics show three out of five taking part in binges.

Alcohol abuse has a grim history that Kinney traces back thousands of years. In AD 81, the abuse of alcohol in ancient Rome was such a problem that the emperor ordered the destruction of all vineyards in Rome. In 1606, being drunk was a statutory offense in England, and a law was enacted called "act for repressing the odious and loathsome sin of drunkenness." In 1620, alcohol came to America on the *Mayflower*. By 1760, Virginia prohibited drinking to excess. In the 1800s, Connecticut passed a law forbidding drinking for more than a half an hour. The temperance movement of the 1800s was born from six drunkards in Chase's tavern in Baltimore who denounced drinking and called for reform. In 1840, the term "alcoholism" was born. It was called a disease in 1900, and by 1919, our nation tried Prohibition to make consumption of alcohol a crime. Once that failed, drink was allowed to flow freely with almost no restraint. By 1971, the National Institute of Alcohol Abuse and Alcoholism (NIAAA) was established to educate society on the risks of alcohol. Clearly, we have fought the negative consequences of alcohol for centuries.

Even the Bible advises control and moderation in the use of alcohol. "Do not get drunk on wine, which leads to debauchery. Instead, be filled with the Spirit"(Ephesians 5:17–19) Another verse says, "Be stunned and amazed, blind yourselves and be sightless; be *drunk*, but not from wine, stagger, but not from beer (Isaiah 29:8–10).

Today we are still contending with this problem, except now our children are also at high risk. Statistics tell us the sad truth that the abuse of drugs and alcohol is the number one health concern for adolescents. How have we as a society failed to learn after so many years of warnings, education, and sorrowful stories? How can it be the leading cause of injury and death for our young people? How can we allow it to cause parent after parent to lie awake, worrying where their teenagers are? How can so many young adults be plagued with alcohol addiction?

Parents themselves often seem to be a contributing factor to the "perfect storm" in that they seem clueless about their own teen's behavior. In our work on the Skaneateles PACT committee, we brought in author Milton Creagh to speak to students. I was sitting in the back of the assembly when Creagh asked the body of high school students, "Who here has lied to their parents?"

Every hand went up. It was a reality check. So much is hidden from parents to "protect us." Our kids do not want to disappoint us, so they live this underground life.

I have worked with Integra, a drug-testing company in Syracuse lead by Chris DePerno, a retired drug enforcement detective. He often has to face down skepticism from parents. While explaining the current trend among teenagers to get the latest high right from their own medicine cabinet with their parents' prescription drugs—crushing drugs such as Oxycontin and then snorting or ingesting them—one parent retorted, "Our kids don't use drugs or alcohol." Yet DePerno challenged parents by recommending "prehab" instead of "rehab." This means parents get pre-educated to recognize the symptoms of alcohol and drug abuse rather than stand in denial. Parenting is not for the faint hearted, and learning how to parent well is always a voluntary choice in our culture. One guidance counselor recently complained that the parenting course she runs every year had no takers—for the first time in her career.

The PACT committee's biggest challenge has not been booking national speakers with vibrant messages but rather getting local parents to be interested enough to fill the auditorium. In our society, it is not a priority to attend drug and alcohol education. Many parents today are too busy for the important voluntary education they used to sign up for. It is sad because the middle school years are so risky for those *clueless* parents. They have no idea how quickly things can change.

A number of years ago, a son-and-mother speaking team came to Skaneateles. Toren Volkmann, and his mother, Chris, wrote a book called, *From Binge to Blackout.*[24] She was honest about her alcohol-dependent son. He never thought his drinking was a problem because everyone else around him seemed to do it. But when he tried to stop after college, he couldn't. He ended up going into rehabilitation and has worked to stay sober ever since.

I first worried about Toren's drinking when we caught him intoxicated at age fifteen. He seemed to bounce back too fast the next morning, and I wondered if that was a normal reaction. Then, when he repeatedly got into trouble for alcohol use and did not change his behaviors, I was baffled. How could it be so important to him to continue his use when it caused him so many problems? Finally, when he went to rehab, I began to understand his symptoms and learned how addiction to alcohol (or any other drug) has common traits. I could have spotted those red flags years earlier had I been better educated about alcohol abuse.

—Chris Volkmann, mother of Toren
From Binge to Blackout

Further exacerbating the "perfect storm" is the reality that it is extremely difficult to ask your child to go against the grain of society. Some kids drink and smoke because it is what their peers do. No one wants to be alone in life. We all want to fit in. My daughter drank in high school, despite the tragedy our family endured, despite everything I tried to learn, enforce and educate. The peer pressure is incredible.

The first couple years after Matt died, I was absolutely against drinking. I didn't think I ever would drink throughout high school, and I never thought that I would give into peer pressure. But the pressure was there. Perhaps the peer pressure that is exemplified in movies and television isn't as true in real life in that someone is holding a beer to your mouth making you drink, but it is an underlying pressure. If my friends were drinking, and I was going to sit in the corner and not be "one of the crowd," I feared losing my friends. My friends would never have pressured me or blamed me for not drinking because I had suffered such a tragedy, but it was the fact that I was missing out. As I look back on it now, high school would have been so much easier without the pressure to drink. I had to lie to my parents and completely lose their trust from time to time and it broke their heart. It also broke my heart that I would even put that stress on them after the suffering they were currently enduring. But for some reason, needless to say, I drank, and I did it because of peer pressure and the pressure of doing what my friends were doing. I knew the devastation alcohol could cause because I had lived it but little did I know the health risks that accompany underage drinking and the damage I was willingly doing to my body.

—Lindsay Angelillo, Binghamton University

Some teens start drinking and using drugs in middle school. Research shows that the earlier one starts using drugs, the greater the chances for dependence and addiction later in life. The risk of dependency for teens who drink at age fourteen runs four times higher than if they start drinking at twenty-one (Prevention Network, Syracuse, New York). One drug and alcohol counselor said that every one of his clients started drinking as a young teenager. Thus education and heightened awareness must start with young adolescents and their parents. Waiting until high school is too late.

I believe caring parents everywhere are voicing the same questions and struggling with the same concerns. How can we ward off this "perfect storm"? What can we do for ourselves and for our children?

Since I started down my long road toward recovery and toward understanding, the key advice I have consistently heard is "stay connected and stay alert." To stay connected and create that "family" feeling and earn your teenager's confidence so they allow you access to their inner life takes time and perseverance. My husband makes me smile and reminds me what it takes to create those bonds. Through his own hobbies, he's walked alongside his kids, teaching them to love the outdoors, hunt, and fish. He loves all sports, and so do they. He is an artist that paints pictures and carves ducks, so they try their hand as well. They all love to cook, as I do, but Lindsay is the best. She also follows my lead on picture taking and video production. Together we come around these activities and passions as a family to play, to enjoy life, to persevere through adversity, and to bond with our hearts.

One of my favorite messages about parenting and family came from Bob Stutman of the Stutman Group, a speaker on drug and alcohol abuse. Stutman references the numbers one through seven and says the higher the number, the less chance your child will abuse drugs or alcohol. You wonder, *What is he talking about?* Then it makes sense: it is the number of nights you eat together as a family. Bingo! The more nights you spend time interacting, communicating and sharing, the better off your child will be. Do it! Eat some meals together! Take your child fishing or dancing!

The other half of staying connected is staying alert. Know where your teenagers are, what they are doing, and with whom they are doing it. This message came across strongly in the video *You Can't Afford to be Clueless* that Prevention Network had produced. It is important to know your children's friends and their parents. This suggestion is respectfully appropriate "because it is a privilege to be a member of a family" as one therapist expressed to Marc and me.

Marc and I hosted many teen functions for Lindsay's class. What worked best was the communication between parents. Many of us were committed to drug- and alcohol-free homes and frequently checked to make sure that a parent was supervising. When I asked my daughter what would help kids say no to alcohol or drugs, she advised, "The parents need to make it very hard to use. Then we would eventually give up." Parents coming together and forming a network of communication and supervision will help prevent opportunities to use.

> It will take all of us to impact the alcohol culture. Here is what I have found to be important: Start dialogue with kids early about alcohol. Remember that alcohol is not

a benign substance and learn about the consequences of youth alcohol abuse. Do not perceive underage and binge drinking as inevitable. Parents can combat the way media portrays alcohol as glamorous. Don't be afraid to ask questions about alcohol use or to seek professional help early if problems arise. *Parents are the most listened-to resource by teens in alcohol decision-making.* Never give up.

—Chris Volkmann
From Binge to Blackout[25]

One fact I learned from my years of working with Prevention Network is that parental expectations, well communicated, are a huge prevention factor. The clearer the parents' expectations are, the less likely their teen will be a "user." Research shows that if you are not clear, your teen will interpret your "lack of clarity" as permission to use. (Prevention Network handout, *Five Strategies That Work*)

I interviewed one student who declared herself free from drugs and alcohol. I asked her what has kept her so strong. The answer was simple, "I don't want to disappoint my mom." Ongoing communication between parent and teen is essential. One student from Skaneateles went on to write an article in college called "Communication Is Key in Curbing Underage Drinking."[26] Kati Card suggests, "With graduations and proms approaching, parents need to sit down with their children and spell out exactly what is acceptable and unacceptable and come to some sort of agreement or compromise." Kati further advises parents, "Always go with your gut instinct. If you feel something is off, different, or just plain not right, you are probably correct." She says, "It comes down to one thing, simply communication, communication between parents and their children. I believe the lack of communication is the root where all problems begin."

Parents can also utilize real-life stories in the news as teachable moments. The deaths of Michael Jackson and Whitney Houston are just two of the many public examples of how difficult it is to overcome addiction. All the money in the world could not change their destinies. As *Fox News* host Bill O'Reilly wrote,[27]

> Houston, however, was an adult who made a decision to embrace the drug life. Reports say she tried to rehabilitate herself a few times, but you know how that goes. Once a person enters the hell of addiction, there is no easy way out.
>
> And that's how the Whitney Houston story should be covered…as a cautionary tale…as another life vanquished by substance abuse.
>
> —Bill O'Reilly, Associated Press

Thirdly, whether it suits us or not, we as parents are the unceasing role models for our children. Our children are always watching us, our behavior, our attitudes, and our talk. We are never off duty. Our behavior toward alcohol directly affects how our children will perceive its importance and eventually use it. I am reminded of our first PACT function where Marc and I shared our hearts to an audience in Skaneateles. Marc said, "How can we ask our kids not to drink and drive if we do?" Marc told the audience he made a deal with Alex. "If you don't drink and drive, I won't either."

Soon after Matt's accident, Marc publicly acknowledged in court and was later quoted in the papers labeling our son's tragedy "a consequence of no consequences." And he was so right! Too many incidences of underage drinking went without consequences in our community, and Marc and I were part of that mind-set. We agree that we should have done more in the area of parenting by staying on top of Matt's activities and communicating clearer expectations. We regret not better educating ourselves about how to handle a "strong-willed child." We regret not following through on discipline. We regret not knowing where Matt was on the evening of June 19, 2004. Our boundaries with Matt were fuzzy and sometimes nonexistent. We thought he would always tell the truth, which he didn't.

Henry McCloud and John Townsend, authors of *Boundaries*, put it simply,[28]

> You reap what you sow. Life is about a natural cause and effect. We will learn from our consequences. It is important to allow our children to suffer natural consequences from their behavior. If we step in to interrupt this natural cause and effect, we are then rescuing them and becoming "codependents." Interrupting the natural consequences of their actions and taking the consequence from them, will disable them from learning true responsibility. We are ultimately harming them."
>
> —*Boundaries: When to Say YES, When to Say NO,*
> *To Take Control of Your Life*

Milton Creagh, has made a huge impact on my understanding of better ways to parent teenagers. His particular emphasis is about how to build character and responsibility into our children so they grow up to be solid, dependable adults. The idea for his book, *Nobody Wants My Child*, came from working with employers who begged, "Give me senior citizens, give me the disabled, but please don't give me teenagers. They are not responsible!" During one high school assembly, he asked the students in the audience, "How many of you mow your lawn?" Only a few hands went up. Creagh vehemently urges parents not to give their children everything but rather teach them how to work, making sure they have responsibilities in the family from the time they are young children: emptying the trash, making simple lunches, feeding the dog. Responsibility starts at home. Once, while addressing an audience of students, I mentioned Matthew's desire to serve his country by attending the United States Air Force Academy and Alex's decision to attend the United States Naval Academy. Then I said, "You do not have to put on a military uniform to serve this great country. You can serve it by working hard and being highly functional in our society."

Since losing Matt, alcohol has become painful and confusing to me. If I could wish it all away—as if longing for the day alcohol never existed—that would be fine. But alcohol is not going away because we are human and we drink. There is something right about a cold beer on a hot day with friends or family or a glass of red wine with my pasta dinner. That's okay with me. That's how we were supposed to use alcohol. It was meant to accompany a meal or be used socially in small quantities and with restraint. It was not meant to cause drunkenness or debauchery, abuse or neglect. It was not meant to create crime and dysfunction. We were supposed to use it in a balanced way: "Everything in moderation." I don't ever want to glorify it or need it in order to be "me." I just want to enjoy it for what it is: a beverage. As a good friend said, "We need to stop thinking that being drunk is funny." When I speak at a "victim impact panel," I am often uncomfortable. The DWI offenders could be my friends, neighbors, or family members. Who am I to judge peers? Years ago, this could have been me, before my fatal vision kicked in. But my goal with these audiences is to plead to the young adults who never had a consequence before and convince them that "wisdom diminishes beer by beer"(Robert Borris, Syracuse DWI Policeman).[29]

With a blood alcohol concentrate (BAC) level of .08 in your blood, it is illegal to drive. Understanding how alcohol impacts your own body should be a required precursor to drinking. I know one glass of wine makes me tired and relaxes me immediately. I may talk too much after two. A third glass would make me feel sick in the morning. The human body needs approximately one hour to absorb and process one serving of alcohol. For some, that means one or two servings of alcohol because it depends on how much you eat, how big you are, and whether you are male or female. This includes one twelve-ounce beer or a five-ounce glass of wine. The only thing that can absorb alcohol is time. I would never drive after one glass of wine unless hours had passed. Coffee, food, or exercise will not speed up this process. I knew a friend who got a DWI in the morning after a hard night of drinking. She had so much to drink that a few hours of sleep was not enough to process the alcohol in her body. In the morning, she was still legally drunk.

Research suggests a drunk driver with a BAC above .08 passes us every few minutes in America. Statistics on the Mothers Against Drunk Driving (MADD) website say an average person drinks and drives eighty times before getting caught. Someone dies in an alcohol related crash every fifty two minutes in our country.[30]

I never want to lose another child or loved one to a drunk driver, so I do what I know I can. I can share Matt's story, I can be a good role model, and I can do my part to not glorify alcohol. I can vow to not drink and drive. If I choose to drink, I can use a designated driver. I can learn how alcohol affects my body. I can help educate others as much as I can. I can impart a type of fear surrounding the stigma of alcohol. I can ignite awareness at every chance I get. I can also try to get help for those who need it.

My hope for change has come from *The Tipping Point*, by Malcolm Gladwell. Gladwell describes times in history when our society grew intolerant of certain behaviors and decided to change. As an example, I tell my audiences how I used to clean my house every Saturday morning for my parents. One of the things I did was clean the ashtrays. Years ago, it would be commonplace to walk into someone's home, ask for an ashtray, and light up a cigarette. It is quite different today. Today, people would be appalled if someone smoked in their home. We never have ashtrays lying around anymore. This change is real and is a result of reaching a tipping point of intolerance to the smell of smoke and the risk of cancer. I tell DWI offenders that the real goal in ten years is for people to be appalled if someone ever drinks and drives. It would be awesome to finally reach that tipping point of total intolerance for driving under the influence and complete disdain for not having a designated driver.

I believe we are finally waking up from a deep denial about the chaos that drugs and alcohol have created in our country. I believe it is up to us because we can do it, not as clueless parents, but as empowered adults. We can change society's beliefs about the importance of alcohol and relegate it to just another beverage choice, which would be socially unacceptable and embarrassing to abuse whether you are a teenager or an adult.

I have said to teens how each generation is different and decides what their generation is intolerant of. So what will the next generation tackle?

I Hope You Dance

I Hope You Dance

As my children walk out the door to attend a high school or middle school dance, I would always say "I hope you dance." When they come home I always ask "Did you dance?" and am overjoyed when they say "Yes."

—Marianne Angelillo
July 29, 2008

Dance has always been a part of my life. I remember back to the first boy/girl dances in the seventh and eighth grades when we were all learning to box dance with the opposite sex for the first time. I remember dancing and singing in a crowd of friends to "Sweet Caroline" in the '70s. I remember dancing to Bruce Springsteen in college, disco dancing to "Saturday Night Fever," and then country dancing to "Urban Cowboy." To me, dancing always involved happiness, friends, and a good time. In my life, it's been synonymous with health, friendship, confidence, and contentment.

Matt was the dancer in my family. You could say he danced through life, embracing every day with a plan for the next minute or hour. He was surrounded by friends always and packed it all in. I would watch him from a distance and feel so content about the son who was so like me. He truly gave it his all. I have photos of him with friends dressed up at dances, in Halloween costumes, always smiling and happy. I never worried about Matt's confidence and happiness because he danced, always.

When Matt's dance of life ended on June 19, 2004, at the age of seventeen, our life instantly ended as we had known it. Everything changed for Matt's three siblings and my husband and me. It has been difficult to dance since Matt died. The lightheartedness, contentment, and peace we had as a family vanished. We tried to stay away from parties and celebrations, always grieving our beloved son, and feeling the hole that would never go away. The dance we had experienced in life seemed to be over for us.

In 2005, I produced a video in my son's memory. I put beautiful video clips of his life to the Garth Brook's song called "The Dance." The significant part of the song is when Garth sings, "If I didn't have the pain, I wouldn't have had the dance." The dance we experience in life should be cherished regardless of how long it lasts or how painful it is when it ends. My husband says Matt packed it all into a seventeen-year lifetime. Now I know that since we never know what the future holds, we need to dance whenever we get the chance.

I experienced grief again, though on a different scale, when my beloved father, friend, and companion passed away in 2008. I missed him terribly and again felt a disconnection from those around me. The pain was different from Matt, as one expects to lose a parent—the natural sequence of life. My father had experienced everything, with a legacy of six children, seventeen grandchildren and six great-grandchildren. Who could complain about saying good-bye to a life like this?

As I built a video slideshow for one more funeral, I felt a true loss. My dad adored and cherished me my whole life. I was losing a fan, a beloved friend, and a companion on so many visits. I had shared my dad with the village of Skaneateles, the town of Exton, the University of Delaware and my high school friends. What a void he was leaving.

He was eighty-four and had a wonderful, full, long life rich with relationships and family. After his death, a package arrived in the mail that made me curious about the enclosed DVD and why it was sent to me. It was labeled "family videos 1967." I popped it into the DVD player and proceeded to watch memories unfold of my parents on vacation with all their friends over forty years ago. The faces were all familiar including family and friends, many who are now deceased. The memories transported me to the best times of my parents' lives, including the good old days of children, friendship, vacations, and celebrations. I proceeded to watch my dad dance at a luau all dressed up in a Hawaiian outfit. He was smiling and laughing and having a great time. They were all dancing and laughing to the rhythm of friendship and happiness and contentment.

The tears I cried were for so many reasons including the loss of my parents, the loss of the dance in my own family, and the gratitude that I did dance for almost forty-seven years before my heart was broken. I looked at the video with a new hope and vision. I want to dance for my dad. I want him to see me dance again. I am ready to learn new dances and dance with new friends. I want to dance at all my children's weddings, as I know they so want to do this with me.

Later that month in 2008, my husband and I attended a wedding of a good old friend of ours. Many friends from our old life of fifteen years ago in Pennsylvania were there. Our good friend, Butch, was in his wheelchair and I watched as the bride proceeded to get him on the dance floor. All the friends surrounded him as he was able to move his arms and shoulders to the music. He operated his wheelchair, and we did a dance around his chair. It was an amazing moment for all of us. We felt gratitude for this opportunity to once again dance together. My friend showed true courage and strength. He was learning to live again and embrace his new life. His wife was by his side and so were all his friends. He was truly dancing at that moment.

I want my family to dance again. It is time. Matthew wants all of us to experience the dance in life. He would be sickened to know that we all gave up dancing because of him. My dad wants the same for me as the daughter who is most like him. I see him and Matt prodding us on and ready to watch us. We get one chance at this dance of life and despite the sadness of our loss, we need to wake up every day and keep dancing for ourselves and each other. The dance is life, is living and cherishing what you have. Dancing is loving and gratitude. We need to say at the end of the day and at the end of a lifetime that we gave it all we got and we truly danced. I do not want to leave this world knowing I did not give it my all. I will do this in memory of my son, my parents, and in the hope of my future with my husband and children.

May God bless us in the dance of life.

Rebuilding

Love of the outdoors has always been a passion for Marc and me. Some of our first dates involved a ride along a river, a picnic by a lake, and a back-pack camping trip. Some of my fondest memories involve Marc taking care of me in nature. He was always his authentic self in the woods, whether hunting with his German shorthaired pointer or making coffee by a campsite.

So the decision in 1994 to buy an old dilapidated hunting camp in Marathon, New York, was fitting to our family and our marriage. We piled the kids into the car and took off that January to see Bloody Pond and ice fish with Marc's good friend, Tim, who also owned a camp on the lake. All four kids—ages three, five, seven, and ten years—were bundled to the hilt. The snow was piled four feet high, and we were mesmerized by the nature of Central New York. Wild turkeys combed the side of the road and majestic hills were everywhere. I felt so passionate for this new part of the world. We drilled our holes for fishing, and the small lake had at least eighteen inches of ice.

Journal entry, January 1994

Matt jumped on a 4-wheeler parked by our ice fishing holes and wanted so bad to turn the key. I said, "No, Matt," and in his Matt headstrong manner, challenged me with, "I'm doing it!"

The kids were as thrilled as we, so we made a family decision to buy this "dump," as I labeled it. The roof was caving in, the structure was leaning, the attic was filled with bats, the plumbing didn't work, and it was filled with old furniture from a couple named "Aunt Pearl and Uncle Wayne." Marc reassured me that we were not buying a home; we were buying a lifestyle. The deed came with lifetime hunting and fishing privileges. This would be where our family would spend quality time together. More conversation happened here over a campfire with my children than anywhere else in life. We spent years making it livable. The kids helped paint it. We ridded it of bats and made it another home.

Journal Entry August 5th, 1996

> This little cabin of ours has become quite a place of solace for us. We so love it here, just us, not bothering anyone else, no TV, no one criticizing us or telling us how to raise our children. We are such a unit here, something right from heaven, such simple abundance.
>
> I don't think about money or entertainment other than nature. I love my front porch, my hummingbirds, my beautiful cottage garden, my wonderful bed to sleep in every night, my camera, my family, my husband and all of our memories. Oh yes, and all the wonderful friends and family who appreciate it with us and also love it! We will always share our simple abundance and hope to spread our "wealth."
>
> I can say it might have been luck to send this cabin and lifestyle our way. However I believe it was God sending it to Marc and I knowing it would enrich our marriage— perhaps save it in a lot of ways.

Marc and I have set a new goal. We have decided to rebuild the family camp for our children, grandchildren, and especially for us. This place of comfort and beauty holds so many wonderful memories.

The camp at Bloody Pond is where we have retreated, time and time again, to recover from a difficult incident or frame of mind. I remember back to one painful car ride home from visiting Alex at Annapolis. Between sad music, painful Matt conversation, and leaving Alex, Marc and I were in a difficult way. When we neared the Marathon exit, I just said, "Let's go to the camp." We pulled in, sat on the couch, and cried together. It felt comfortable and familiar to be where we spent so much time as a family. After regrouping, Marc said, "This was a good idea."

Marc and I have found an inner peace at Bloody Pond, and so we have tried to spend more time there. It seems fitting that the desire to rebuild our marriage and life coincides with rebuilding Bloody Pond. Before we knocked down our camp, we found time to empty out seventeen years of memories. I packed all the old camp photos into a box and scanned them for a memory book. In one photo, Matt is holding up a seventeen-inch bass, in another he's sitting by a fire with the deer-hunting crew, smiling with his buddies, including his best friend, Alex.

There are many wonderful moments to remember, and we were blessed to have seventeen years with Matt. Our loss was horrific, but we learned how to truly keep Matthew close. He lives on in our hearts, and he will live on in our new camp. He lives on in each of his siblings and in his friends who will never forget him.

In 2010, as the construction workers were hammering nails into new walls, Marc hung Matt's Mass card over the blueprints. This place will be called "the camp at Bloody Pond," but it comes at a great expense. We decided to use the money from the wrongful death settlement to help pay for the construction. This was the most unwanted money anyone would ever receive. We would give it back a million times to have our son with us. That was not God's plan. So we sought a way to restore peace in Matt's absence. The summer we rebuilt this new camp renewed hope and passion in my family. We planned rooms, looked through books, and resurrected an old thrill similar to fixing up our first home, back in Pennsylvania. This time, it is for our grandchildren and children. We want them to have this gift from their brother.

Christmas eve of 2011 Marc and I presented the children with a beautiful bronze plaque to hang by the front door.

> Angelillo Camp
> Established 1994
> Rebuilt 2010
> For Marc, Alex and Lindsay
> With love from your brother Matthew

Our Christmas of 2011 brought no tears. A wonderful family gathered at the new camp to open presents and eat Christmas Eve dinner. We talked and laughed by a fire, and we reminisced about old times. I gave Marc a new book of memories, including construction photos of the new camp. I included pictures of our new friends, the Andy Hull Construction Company crew. I also included many old friends who had stopped by to check on our progress. I know they look forward to spending time with us at our new camp.

I received a card from my husband on our thirtieth anniversary. He said, "As we go forward together, I want to continue to love you forever and enjoy all the blessings we have had bestowed on us, including our time with Matt." This is a true blessing for me. Marc and I no longer just see the "hole" left by our son. It took a very long time and many years, but we are seeing a future, and we are grateful for the memories left to us by our beloved son.

In our own ways, we each are moving on. My son, Marc IV, worked hard after college, finding a good job and his own apartment in Albany. He stayed close to Marc and me by coming home on weekends to help with the rebuilding of Bloody Pond. He built patios, walkways, and the stonework on the chimney. In the fall of 2010, he decided to move to Texas for a career in the industrial pump business. Marc and I had a tough time saying that final goodbye, but this is what we all wish for our children, isn't it? We raise them to be independent, responsible, and loving with their own dreams and goals. My husband and I are proud of the young man Marc has become. I look forward to all his frequent visits back to Central New York. It is in his blood and I find comfort knowing that he loves it here.

We witnessed Alex graduate from the Naval Academy and beamed with pride as he accepted his diploma from the United States Secretary of Defense, Robert Gates. Alex worked hard majoring in mechanical engineering and graduated first in his class academically. My guess is that he did it for Matt. "Go for it," his brother told him nine years ago, and he listened. I know the work was not easy. He questioned the commitment during his plebe year in 2007, wondering if it was right for him. I knew he felt pressure after Matt's death to fulfill the military academy commitment his brother started in 2003. But one day he told his dad, "I may have gone for you, but I am staying for me." It was music to our ears that his path was fitting more clearly into his future.

> Matt always pushed me to be the best. He believed in my potential, and would never let me settle for anything less than full effort. I took his words to heart, striving for excellence in and out of school. I have him to thank for giving me the motivation to challenge myself and come to the Academy.
>
> — *Alex Angelillo*
> "Amor Fratrium"

The young challenged plebe of six years ago is now an officer in the United States Navy. In February of this year, Alex married his devoted high school sweetheart, Andrea. Andrea had supported him throughout his four years at the academy while getting a nursing degree at the University of Maryland. They are stationed in Washington State while Alex is on active duty.

Lindsay finished her senior year at Binghamton, loving her friends, and excited about a business degree. She is maturing, and I do accept and understand her love of dancing and jovialness. She is so much like Matt and me, always wanting to be with people. Recently, she brought some college friends home for a few days and introduced them to life in Skaneateles. I came home one night to find them watching the family graduation videos. She loves her brothers and is proud of her life with them. We ended the evening by showing "the Matthew Angelillo story." The crumpled red Ferrari, the judge in a Syracuse courtroom, and a beautiful boy jumping off cliffs filled the screen. Tears were streaming down her roommates' faces, and they surely would have loved to meet this brother, Matt.

Our relationship with Lindsay has been challenged by underage drinking. In college, Lindsay was clearly in charge of her own decisions regarding alcohol. However, one experience helps comfort my heart that I have done everything possible to influence her. I had an opportunity to speak at LeMoyne College in Syracuse for Drug and Alcohol Awareness Week. Unfortunately, there were few attendees. However, I noticed a group of students coming down the aisle. I soon recognized the leader as my beautiful "bearcat" daughter, Lindsay. She had brought six of her friends. It did not surprise me that she would want to share "the Matthew Angelillo story" with her friends. Lindsay has struggled with the inner conflict of our tragedy and society's pressure to drink. I wrote to her afterwards.

Dear Lindsay,

You are an incredibly supportive daughter and I thank you. It was so sweet of you to bring your friends last night and drive all that way! I hope I came across all right to you and your friends, please feel free to critique so I can get better. Was it terribly hard for you? You are so strong and amazing! And thank you for letting me share and not shutting me down. I appreciate you every moment of my life! I love you...

Mom

And her response:

Mom

It was absolutely my honor to bring my friends and hear you talk about our wonderful family, despite the hardships we have faced. I honestly do not feel pain when I hear about Matt or hear you talk about him, I feel blessed that I knew him the thirteen years of my life that I did. He was an amazing person and that is because you and Dad are amazing parents. I am so appreciative of you and all that you and Dad do for me. I honor how strong you are. My friends were blown away by your speech and the video. Keep up the good work Mom. I can promise you that seven people sitting in that audience will never drink and drive and will always think about their families before doing something reckless. I love you!

Lindsay

Lindsay and I have been able to share a glass of wine or two since she turned twenty-one. We have danced at a few country concerts while sipping our sole beer of the night. We both know that our relationship is a solid healthy one. She respects my opinions regarding alcohol and has even actively participated in this book. Each week, she would review a chapter and offer her critiques. I respect her as a daughter and friend. I look forward to the many smiles she will bring me.

So another child leaves the nest. Lindsay moved to New York City this summer to begin her career in business. We are both so excited for this chapter of her life and I cannot wait to visit while I watch her grow as an individual and employee.

Peace has been restored to the Angelillo family, and I am forever grateful for respite from the chaos in our lives. I realize it may only be temporary, but I am truly enjoying it anyway. I asked Alex if he still had bad moments, and for all of us, the answer is the same—yes, bad moments are a part of loss, the grief, and the heartache of losing someone so special. Matt is in our family forever. Nothing will ever take him from us and we will each remember him in our own ways.

But most of all, I thought back to our time together, to that December day in the Brigantine…

The North wind seemed colder after hours of uneventful duck hunting, of futilely calling to birds in their formation miles high, of enjoying only the hot chocolate in our thermos and the powdered donuts we bought at the Wawa. It cuts through every layer and chills our bones. We sit in dejection when, in the distance, we hear the whistling wings of a lone duck. My dad fumbles with his calls; his first note squeals through the moisture which has by now frozen inside. He chuckles the "feeding call," and the duck cannot resist. A pintail! For years, we spoke of when we would get our first pintail; we became fascinated with this duck my dad spoke of so fondly. With wings locked, it sails into our spread, preparing to splash down among the decoys when the three of us rise from our hidden lair. Pushing through the reeds which conceal us, we let loose thunderous blasts from our shotguns which drop the bird "stone-dead" in the water. As Mavis leaps forth into the frigid waters to retrieve him, we can not help but enjoy our moment. Mavis brings it back to the boat; it is in perfect condition, and is beautiful. Surely, Dad will mount it for us. It does not matter that we do not see anything for the next hours; we still tap our feet in restrained ebullience. Now we have stories of pintails in the Brigantine to tell our sons. I look to my right, and a smile comes across Matt's lips.

—*Alex Angelillo*
"Amor Fratrium"

The hole is still there. We see it and we feel it, but we choose life. We choose love. We choose family and we use every ounce of courage given to us.

I recently had a dream about Matt. I was in an emergency room, having some sort of heart problem and was upset that Matt was out there somewhere, homeless and alone. I asked my husband if we could go find Matt. *We have to find Matt!* Marc agreed and said yes, "let's go find him." I was so hopeful to find Matt and said, "Let's go now!" Then I woke up. I cried upon awakening because once again, there was no hope. There's no more hope for finding Matt in this life. Many parents have lost their children temporarily, but they can hope that someday, they will get them back. In death, there's no return. They are "gone4ever."

So I present my school assemblies and attend my Bible studies. I know Matt is as close to me as my other children. I told a recently bereaved mother that after nine years, my mind still goes to thoughts of my four children equally. Matt is never shortchanged by not being here physically. He is thought of each and every day, as are his siblings. I know his life has been used for the good in this world, and someday we will be reunited in the next.

Last year, a wonderful family in our community lost their twenty-six-year-old son. I asked my partner in grief, Jeanette, to sit with Lisa and me. I took them to my favorite spot, "mother's mourning" on the lake, and we talked for hours. She cried and cried and asked, "Did you want to die?" We both instantaneously said, "Yes, we did want to die, but we don't want to now."

Jeanette and I moved through years of suffering, grief, and confusion but now are graced by peace offered by family and friends. We both have rich lives filled with love and hope and faith. We have accepted the death of our sons and are now teaming up to give someone else hope that this pain will soften someday.

One year after the tragic loss of Lisa's son, we gathered again at the new camp. We talked about a sign from our sons that they are okay. Lisa pleaded, "I just wish he would send me a sign!" Jeanette responded with a smile and said, "I can just see our three sons up there laughing at us. They are frustrated saying, "We sent them each other, we sent them a beautiful day, and we sent them hummingbirds, a Baltimore oriole, and this camp. Isn't that enough of a sign for them?"

No family should ever have to walk in our shoes. It is bad enough that life deals blows beyond our control, such as cancer, accidents, war, and unavoidable tragedies. However, teenage fatalities due to bad choices are avoidable. As a society, we do everything to get people to live forever—or at least to a hundred! We sob at our grandparents' funerals, thinking that age seventy-eight was too young. I know now that seventeen is way too young. Matt was robbed of his life, and so were all of us.

I want the world to know how important all teenagers are! I want to be a part of awakening our culture to work harder to save our teens from senseless risk taking. It is my mission to use Matt's soul and my family's journey to continue the impact that Matt should have made in person.

Yes, it is *up to us*! Each day, we have an opportunity to do it better! I realize how much has changed in my own community over the past eight years. Syracuse and Skaneateles are trying. Prevention Network and John Underwood are trying. The athletes who take part in Honor the Code are trying. Denis Foley is trying. My children are trying. Marc and I are trying. It is not easy, but real change starts with each of us having open minds and faith to believe that change really can happen.

I do believe that we all are here to connect, encourage and learn from each other. This cannot happen without *sharing our stones*. We need to be aware of the faces behind the tragedies, and through my story, I have offered you a face that is precious to me, my beautiful son. Each tragedy our country endures represents another face to be mourned and another stone to be shared. I believe that as we put faces to our tragedies, we are educating others and therefore tipping points of significant change can happen sooner. I am hoping that someday one of my grandchildren will be able to say to me, "Grandma, are you telling me that people would actually drink and then drive a car?" I am also hoping that society will become a bit more patient and willing to take some stones from others who are bereaved, sick, or just sad. It is my fervent desire to encourage more compassion and understanding. Father McGrath's explanation of Jesus' parable of the sower, spoken at Matt's funeral in June 2004, inspired me to use my own words to plants seeds of hope and change by *sharing my stones*. It is my prayer that my words fall on "good soil."

It's the parable of the sower:

Again Jesus began to teach by the lake. The crowd that gathered around him was so large that he got into a boat and sat in it out on the lake, while all the people were along the shore at the water's edge. He taught them many things by parables, and in his teaching said: "Listen! A farmer went out to sow his seed. As he was scattering the seed, some fell along the path, and the birds came and ate it up. Some fell on rocky places, where it did not have much soil. It sprang up quickly, because the soil was shallow. But when the sun came up, the plants were scorched, and they withered because they had no root. Other seed fell among thorns, which grew up and choked the plants, so that they did not bear grain. Still other seed fell on good soil. It came up, grew and produced a crop, some multiplying thirty, some sixty, some a hundred times."

Then Jesus said, "Whoever has ears to hear, let them hear."

"My good people, it is that final seed that I would like us to think about this afternoon. It's that final seed that I hope will be operative in this church today, so that the words which God has given to me to share with you, will take root and they will produce fruit, thirty, sixty, and a hundred fold.

And of course that's up to you as individuals.

We have to initiate new beginnings in our lives and so in the process, put an end to the tragic endings that we celebrate today. And it would be a great tragedy continuing if we have not learned something. Our hearts are aching this afternoon because of this senseless mistake, but we have to turn it into something good.

—Father Thomas J. McGrath
Homily delivered at the Mass of
resurrection for Matthew Angelillo

Journal Entry 7/16/11

Yes, my life has been an open book. I have left my writings and journals for the world to see. I have not been ashamed of my difficult journey. It has been a long hard struggle to survive and I would not have made it without all of the love in my life.

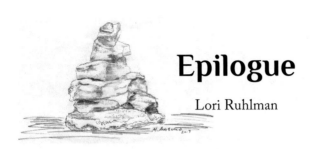

Epilogue

Lori Ruhlman

"One Boy"

One boy goes to court today to face charges of drunk driving.
One boy is buried.

Scores of teenage boys dig into their closets for sports coats and
ties, or borrow their fathers' suits and dress shoes

To wear inside the Catholic church, where they will say a final
goodbye
To the boy they've known all of their lives.

One mother moves through the day, the fourth day without the
boy she loved and raised for seventeen years.

One mother, one block away, grieves for the mother whose boy
is dead
And braces herself to watch her own son put on a suit and step
up to the judge's bench in court

One sister clings to the thought
That her brother's eyes will help someone else to see
And that his organs will help someone else to live.

One sister, a block away, thinks of her brother's horrible mistake

That in one instant
Took away a friend's life forever.

Girls and boys, young men and young women, finish final exams
And think not of the warm summer sun and days on the lake,
But of the boy who will not be there.

One father embraces the boy who drove the car that killed his son
And says bitterness will not bring his own boy back.

One father, a block away, worries about his son's future,
Saying everything he worked so hard for is ruined and that his
    life is over.
But his boy will graduate from high school, have children
And live to grow old.

The boy who is buried today
Will be forever young, blond, and smiling
As he is in the framed photographs by his coffin,
Smiling with the sun on his face and a twinkle in his eye.

As the days, weeks and years go by
His brothers, his sisters and his parents will move on
Without him,
Feeling the quiet bedroom, the empty chair at Thanksgiving,
The opportunities lost,
The grandchildren never born.

His classmates will graduate, move away, go to college.
Some will think of him for the rest of their lives before they get
    into a car
With someone who has been drinking.
Some will toast to his life as they down another beer.
One boy goes to court today.
One boy is buried.

September, 2004

Fall came as always,
Forcing yellow buses back on the roads
And boats back into storage.
The class of 2005 walked through the doors,
Wearing the new confidence of seniors.

But on the athletic fields, in the cafeteria and on the dance floor,
This senior year is different.

The biggest presence
Is felt for the one who is no longer there.

The boy, the jokester, the smart football player, the sometimes-
   mischievous one with the light blue eyes is gone.

His friend, the one who drove the car that flipped and killed him,
Walks into school each day.

He will never be himself again
Because he is, to all who see him, the one who drove after drinking,
The one whose court case is pending
The one whose future is on hold.
What is he to himself?

Does he know that no one can look at him
And see the boy they saw just last spring?

The track star, the good student, the sometimes-bully
In the carefully pressed button-down shirt.

Pictures taken last June freeze the old moments in time.
A line of happy juniors, girls in gowns and boys in suits,
Posing in front of the blue waters of their hometown lake.
Now, even who they were then has changed.

The photographs, shown to observers, have already taken on the
     importance of history.
This is the boy who drove the car.
This is the one we don't hear much about: the one who was
     injured and lived.
And this is the boy who died when the sports car rolled.
So alive in the photo that it is like new, raw hurt to see him there,
Happy, healthy, and unknowing.

Seeing him so naturally there, and then remembering, is like
     having him taken away
All over again.
The boy who died.
The boy who is missing this year
In the hallways, on the football field, in the locker room, at the
     dinner table.

The boy who can't tell us
What he thinks we should do;
What he wishes he had done differently;
What lessons he would like for us to learn.
Only his absence can remind us
How permanent some choices can be.

Afterword

I knew I could never find peace with publishing this book unless I told Steven about it. I contacted him when it was finished and asked him if he would like to read it. I told him that I had always wanted to write a book to share our family's journey. I made sure he knew that I never wanted to hurt him as I included many of the stories of the crash, tragedy, trial, and our relationship. I wanted his blessing and for him to have an opportunity to comment on it.

He came to our door for the first time in almost eight years. I immediately said I was so grateful he wanted to read it. We had a warm exchange, and he took the book home. I waited anxiously for his reaction. A few weeks later, he picked me up and we went out to my favorite spot, the point, with two chairs. We sat for hours and just chatted about everything. Steve graduated from Amherst College, which included his love of running while there. He received an all-American athletic award while on the Amherst track team. He has a job and is still looking for that perfect career.

The discussion about the book was simple. He just said to me, "It's completely fair." I asked him a few questions for clarification but basically felt a huge sense of relief that he was not opposed to the book. He even said there were parts about Matt that made him laugh.

I will leave Steve's journey and story for him to tell. Maybe someday he will write his own book. But this meeting meant so much to me personally. I love Steven. He is Matt's friend and he paid the only price he was able to—the loss of Matt and a prison sentence. I only hope that now life gives him a fair chance to fulfill his own destiny and become the man he is meant to be. This perhaps is the best way to honor his good friend and our beloved son, Matt.

Endnotes

1. "College Drinking: Changing the Culture." *http://www. collegedrinkingprevention.gov/StatsSummaries/snapshot.aspx*. US Government, 1 July 2010. Web. 25 Aug. 2012. <http://www.collegedrinkingprevention.gov/StatsSummaries/snapshot.aspx>.
2. Angelillo, Marc C. "Preparing for Tragedy(title)A father reflects on the meaning of suffering(/title)." *Post-Standard* [Syracuse] 17 Mar. 2005, sec. A: n. pag. Print.
3. Wolterstorff, Nicholas. *Lament of a Son*. Grand Rapids: Wm. B. Eerdmans, 1987. Print.
4. Sittser, Jerry. *A Grace Disguised*. Grand Rapids: Zondervan, 1998. Print.
5. Seely, Hart. "Kids Drink, Someone Dies." *The Post-Standard* [Syracuse] 6 Mar. 2005, Final ed., Final Edition: 1-6. Print.
6. *http://www.hsph.harvard.edu*. http://www.hsph.harvard.edu/cas/rpt2000/CAS2000rpt2.html, 1999. Web. 21 Aug. 2012. <http://www.hsph.harvard.edu/cas/rpt2000/CAS2000rpt2.html>.
7. Angelillo, Marianne. "It Didn't Work." *Post-Standard* [Syracuse] 17 Feb. 2005, Letter to the Editor: n. pag. Print.
8. Angelillo, Marc. "It's up to Us." *Post-Standard* [Syracuse] 11 Jan. 2006, Letter to the Editor: n. pag. Print.
9. Gladwell, Malcolm. *The Tipping Point*. N.p.: Little, Brown and Company, 2002. Print.

10. Kendall, R. T. *Total Forgiveness*. Lake Mary: Charisma House, 2002. Print.

11. Friedell, Dan. "Knowing What a Real Loss Feels Like." *The Citizen* [Auburn] 11 Oct. 2005, A5: n. pag. Print.

12. Young, William P. *The Shack*. Newbury Park: Windblown Media, 2007. Print.

13. *Compassionate Friends*. Compassionate Friends, 12 Oct. 2006. Web. 23 Aug. 2012. <http://www.compassionatefriends. org/CMSFiles/X101206Press_Release_Survey,_Divorce-National.pdf>.

14. McGrath, Thomas J. "Homily delivered at the Mass of resurrection for Matthew Angelillo." Skaneateles Press (Skaneateles) August 2004: n.pag.Print

15. Tozer, A. W. *The Counselor*. Camp Hill: Wingspread, 2009. Print.

16. Bonner, Michael. "Loss drives dedication." *The Citizen* [Auburn, NY] 31 May 2010: n. pag. Print.

17. Angelillo, Marianne. "Hard-hitting video talks to parents." *Skaneateles Journal* [Skaneateles] Sept. 2008: n. pag. Print.

18. Foley, Denis. *Stop DWI*. Lexington, MA: D.C.Heath and Company, 1986. Print.

19. Dohrmann, George, and Jeff Benedict. "Criminal Records in College Football." *Sports Illustrated* 7 Mar. 2011: n. pag. Print.

20. Angelillo, Marianne. "It Didn't Work." *Post-Standard* [Syracuse] 17 Feb. 2005, Letter to the Editor: n. pag. Print.

21. SAMSHA. "Government Study." *SAMSHA* (2010): n. pag. Print.

22. Riera, Michael. *Uncommon Sense for Parents of Teenagers*.

23. O'Martian, Stormie. *The Power of a Praying Woman*. Eugene, OR: Harvest House Publishers, 2007. Print. Power of Praying.

24. Volkmann, Toren, and Chris Volkmann. *From Binge to Blackout*. New York: NAL Trade, 2006. Print.

25. Volkmann, Toren, and Chris Volkmann. *From Binge to Blackout*. New York: NAL Trade, 2006. Print.

26. Card, Kati. "Communication is a key factor in curbing underage drinking." *Fulton Daily News* [Fulton, NY] 9 Aug. 2006: n. pag. Print.

27. O'Reilly, Bill. "Houston's death offers sad lessons drugs." *Press&Sun-Bulletin* [Binghamton, NY] 19 Feb. 2012, sec. 3C: n. pag. Print.

28. Cloud, Henry, and John Townsend. *Boundaries:When to Say Yes, How to Say No to Take Control of Your Life*. Grand Rapids: Zondervan, 2002. Print.

29. Kirst, Sean. "'Top Cop' offers sobering insights into DWI." *The Post-Standard* [Syracuse] 18 Jan. 2006, sec. b: 1+. Print.

30. "Mothers Against Drunk Driving." *Mothers Against Drunk Driving*. MADD, 2012. Web. 9 Dec. 2012. <http://www.madd.org/drunk-driving/about/>.